God Is Just Love

Building Spiritual Resilience and
Sustainable Communities for the Sake
of Our Children and Creation

Ken Whitt

To learn more about this book and its author, please visit
www.GodIsJustLove.com

Cover design and illustration by Rick Nease
www.RickNeaseArt.com

Published by Read the Spirit Books
An imprint of Front Edge Publishing
42807 Ford Road, Suite 234
Canton, MI

Front Edge Publishing books are available for discount bulk purchases for events, corporate use and small groups. Special editions, including books with corporate logos, personalized covers and customized interiors are available for purchase. For more information, contact Front Edge Publishing at info@FrontEdgePublishing.com.

Dedicated To

My children

Stacey
Lauren
Micah
Sally

They are among the many children in my life, including Sandy, Ian,
John, Sara, Gwen, Mackenzie, Audrey, Maxton, Makenna, Kasey,
Alison, Elaina, Morgan, Sekhir and the others
Who are so close to God that through their eyes
I glimpse the Kingdom of God,
On Earth as it is in Heaven.

Contents

Praise for *God Is Just Love*

Ken Whitt presents a fresh perspective for our unprecedented times on spirituality and science. With abundant references to both scripture and science, Ken offers new concepts with nearly every turn of the page. His poetic style makes these concepts accessible and easy to grasp. I especially like the "100 Things Families Can Do to Find Hope and Be Love."

C. Jeff Woods, Interim General Secretary, American Baptist Churches, USA, author, *Better Than Success, 8 Principles of Faithful Leadership*

God Is Just Love is a warm and deeply personal book about a journey into the unconditional love of God—and into a luminous spirituality where science and religion complement each other as paths of understanding that help us to access that Love—in nature, in one another, and especially in our own hearts.

Carl McColman, author of *Unteachable Lessons* and *Befriending Silence*

This book offers a much-needed guide for parents and all of us as we navigate the rising waters of our changing climate. Wonderful stories unfold the path of creative love, courage, spiritual practice and resilience, teaching us how to walk together into future.

Nancy Flinchbaugh, author of *Awakening: A Contemplative Primer on Learning to Sit* **and** *Letters from the Earth*

If you're a parent or Christian educator, tired of false choices between faith and science, Ken Whitt offers this accessible intergenerational resource to help your family or congregation experience God's ever-present love more deeply, and grow in love for—and commitment to—all of our neighbors in God's creation.

Betsy J. Sowers, Minister for Earth Justice, Old Cambridge Baptist Church, Cambridge, MA

Ken Whitt weaves a tapestry of conversations with children, explorations of life in community and dialogue with physicists and theologians of a scientific bent. All of this is part of a quest for hope in a world in which, as he sees it, our children "will encounter grave difficulties." In Whitt's telling, the "singularity"—the original condition which stands at the heart of contemporary cosmology—corresponds to God as "just love": love before, beside and beyond all reality. Our invitation is to embrace the possibilities that emerge from this love and to imagine and create a better future. Whitt's vision is both lyrical and practical, right down to "to do" lists that we can engage as individuals, families and communities.

David L. Wheeler, adjunct professor of theology, Palmer Theological Seminary

To experience Ken Whitt's book is like encountering the author himself. Ken is steeped in his calling as a spiritual leader, which he perceives as companionship. His concern and love for others that began in deep family relationships broadens out to a wide range of connections that manifest in the living of his life. This book is born of that reality. Ken sees the connection of spirituality and science, brilliantly warning of the risks we face if we ignore what is before us and the generations to come. Each chapter moves the reader more deeply into the urgency of recognizing and responding to the call of love that we owe to our children and to our planet. Truly, Ken Whitt is on a journey where God is his guide and his roadmap is "Just Love."

Sister Lois Barton, Retreat Leader for the Sisters of St. Joseph and Program Director of the Sophia Center for Spirituality in Binghamton, New York

Ken Whitt writes this book from the point of view of his Christian faith and experience, yet with openness to the faith and experience of others. He connects many important themes, including the shared truth of spirituality and science while speaking prophetically to current events. In his book Ken describes in easy to understand terms, and with deep compassion for those of us caring for children, how we need to change how we live our daily lives in order to thrive, no matter what happens next. This is a must read for all who have a concern for future generations.

Roger Fritz, retired IBM engineer and Christian lay leader

In a world dominated by specialists, Ken Whitt has invested his life towards becoming a generalist who can see the Big Picture. He connects the dots for his readers between: spirituality and science, history and current events, scripture and experience, past and future, despair and hope, love and justice. Ken makes it possible for us to know and share the Universal Story, the story that answers the big questions: Who are we? Why are we here? What do we do next? This book is a field guide for adults who love children and long to accompany them on their journey through a present and future of ongoing perils. Ken shares the journey he and his family are on and, with a pastor's care, a preacher's passion, and a grandpa's tenderness, invites us to join him in a community seeking to embody Christlike Just Love. This is a hopeful and timely message.

Michael Dowd, author of *Thank God for Evolution* and host of *Post-doom Conversations*

I love how this book explores the depths and heights of God's love, which is infinite and encompasses all that exists way beyond our comprehension, from the beginning to the end of time and eternally. Ken Whitt creatively and profoundly leads us on a journey of examining and understanding what the love of God means for us here and now, and for our children and their children in the future. Thank God that he has the wisdom and the grace to share his own journey of growth toward the glory of God, and may God bless us all with the gifts to dive in and join him in that journey to connect and create a world that is good for everyone. Let us all reflect on his words and then discern and do the actions that arise within us to find hope and be love in this world forever embraced within God's Just Love.

Kate Jacobs, retired pastor and Executive Director of the National Minister's Council, American Baptist Churches, USA

This is a delightful book elegantly written by Ken Whitt, a family man who has attained great wisdom over a long lifetime of experience in ministry, child rearing and grandchild rearing. Reading these pages, you will be touched by Ken's practical insights as he introduces you to the stupendous Cosmic Love Story binding us all together in the One who never ceases to love us unconditionally. In these pages, spirituality and science converge to give a unified world view of the created and emerging universe. Like the Irish philosopher and mystic John Moriarty (1938–2007) did before him, Ken shows how we have been going the wrong way for a long time. Fortunately, Ken sees a hopeful solution in the nurturing and rearing well of the next generation. Indeed, this book is a most useful and practical guide for parents, teachers, grandparents and youth workers to equip young people to face the challenges of the 21st century with confidence and personal effectiveness. Ken illustrates the importance of extended family relationships. He shows how one can easily pass on eternal verities to them in a fun way through family clusters and outings in places of great natural beauty. He shows how the use of songs and rhymes and stories—and the totality of the group dynamic— has a transformative effect on young lives who then learn effortlessly by doing and being. I recommend this practical book to anyone who cares about children and youth development with the highest of endorsement.

Brother Seán Aherne, a Celtic Christian monk living in a small monastery outside Dublin, Ireland, co-editor of *Introducing John Moriarty in His Own Words*

In my several decades as a counselor and spiritual director, it is only in the last five years or so that I have begun to hear a real fear in most of my clients' hearts. Parents are especially fearful of the kind of world their children will be inheriting. As deeply as anyone I know, Ken Whitt has faced these great perils in the world. In his research and personal search, he writes passionately and wisely about how to help ourselves and our children be able to live in a world that most likely is going to be fraught with danger. Ken writes from a great love for his four children and his beautiful grandchildren and a deep care as to how they can survive and even thrive. Ken is both practical and wise and offers deep insights into how to prepare ourselves and our children for the future.

Larry Reichley, Spiritual Director and Counselor

From my point of view of a scientist, an engineer and a Christian, Ken Whitt is a superlative writer. He constantly reaches out with his words that hold me, like: "Christ present in the Jesus of faith, who is as close to me as my breath." And: "Nonetheless, God, Just Love, is running down the field and is about to pass the ball, to you. Be there. It all depends on you. God is Just Love. Be this love." He really believes that "In Christ," Paul's famous dictum, means that we can be the love of God to the world. Most important, he illuminates with stories, songs, prayers, and experiences in creation, the path on which we pass this love to our children. Our children can, in fact, find hope and be love, no matter what comes next.

Dave Allburn, CEO National Fingerprint Companies, retired USAF engineer

"We are loved, and we are equipped to return love." To Ken Whitt, these are both theological assertions and scientific facts. Suspicion and enmity between science and faith will come to an end when faithful people and people of science trust each other and collaborate for the sake of our children and of creation. Ken Whitt declares boldly that the love birthed in the moment of Creation can save humanity from self-absorption, sin and neglect of the environment. Ken Whitt calls for a celebration of the ways of God that have been made known and for the commitment of Christian disciples to anticipate the ways of God yet to be made known. This is a work of consequence.

W. Kenneth Williams, retired pastor and denominational executive of the American Baptist Churches, USA

Foreword

Back in the Before Time, when people used to get on airplanes and go on vacation, my wife Jeanie and I liked to go to the Woodstock Inn, a lovely hotel found at the center of an absolutely charming little Vermont village.

We loved everything about that little town and that hotel. Some years we would go in the fall. If we picked the exact right weekend, the changing leaves would take our breath away. If we went in the winter, we enjoyed the frigid winds, packed snow, horse-drawn sleigh rides and drinks by the fireplace.

I will here publicly admit for the very first time that the thing I loved most about going to this hotel was its high-end spa. (Judge me if you will.) What I loved most about that spa experience was not the massage—okay, this is a close call, but I stand by it—but instead the high-walled outdoor lounge with its heated pool.

You come out of the spa, wrap up in a thick downy-soft robe, and go outside. Maybe it's 20 degrees and sunny, with the sun's faint heat barely felt. But that's okay because you can jump immediately into the heated pool. The part of your body outside the water feels the brisk cold. The part in the water feels the liquid warmth. Every nerve ending tingles happily as massaged skin meets cold and heat and wind and water. Something about the contrasts encountering each other in your one single body creates an out-of-this-world experience.

Reading this book makes me feel a little bit like being in that pool in Woodstock.

How? It feels like self-care, and God himself knows that I need some self-care as I write these words—and probably I am not the only one. Ken Whitt offers care to weary souls in this book. It is not just his words but the spirit that manifests through the words. Ken says that love is at the heart of reality and love is what he gently breathes on us here.

But maybe it is the contrast between the soothing love that he offers and the jangling dangers that he resists that makes this book think of Woodstock Inn. This is a book about finding hope in and for our children and grandchildren but also about naming the dangers that deeply threaten them.

So maybe that is why this book makes me feel like the spa at Woodstock Inn. It is about the contrasts, as they interact with each other—dark skies, bright light; freezing cold, comforting warmth; desperate times, grounded hope. In the end, Ken persuades me that hope in a God of Just Love gets the last word.

Take care of yourself. Find new hope. Read this book.

David P. Gushee
October 11, 2020

David P. Gushee is Distinguished University Professor of Christian Ethics and Director of the Center for Theology and Public Life at Mercer University. He is Past-President of both the American Academy of Religion and Society of Christian Ethics. He is the author and/or editor of 24 books, including Changing Our Mind.

Preface

When I first met Ken Whitt, I was struck by how much we have in common.

First and foremost, we are people centered in faith that expresses itself in just love. Each of us, having served for many years as a pastor, has had time to sift out a lot of religious chaff—and shift our focus to the essential spiritual grain. We've reached the same conclusion that Paul reached in Galatians (5:6): The only thing that matters is faith expressing itself through love.

Second, we are both proud grandfathers. There's something that happened to me when my kids had kids: I found myself less interested in my own success and more interested in theirs. My horizon widened, so that I thought not just in terms of my own lifespan, but theirs. I sensed this same shift in Ken. As dads, we raised our kids for 18 years or so, but at every step they have been raising us too, and we have received far more from our kids and grandkids than we have been able to give.

Third, we love both the outdoors and the Bible, and we see them as two complementary channels of revelation and inspiration. Our many years of interpreting each in light of the other has led us to a more contemplative approach to faith and life, centered in values like the ones Ken celebrates in this book: love, wonderment, and diversity.

And finally, we both love to write. I remember one of my literature professors who regularly quoted the Latin poet Horace on the purpose of poetry: to instruct and to delight. If we delight without instruction, we only amuse. If we instruct without delight, we bore. But if we can put the two together, we help people develop a taste for joy and wisdom.

As you read this wise and joyful book, I know you will feel both instructed and delighted, and you will agree that your life has been enriched by adopting Ken Whitt as a literary pastor, mentor and friend.

Brian McLaren is an author, speaker, activist and public theologian. A former college English teacher and pastor, he is a passionate advocate for "a new kind of Christianity" that is just, generous and working with people of all faiths for the common good. He is the author of more than 20 books.

Introduction

"Wow, you're here, too!" That's what I said as I met Ken Whitt on the picket line in Boston protesting the nuclear arms race and calling for a nuclear freeze. Ken and I knew each other through connections in our denomination. We didn't know each other well, but enough to recognize and greet each other at regional meetings. Yet I was surprised to see him on the picket line for peace, which reveals the sometimes-fractured way we experience our faith and social concerns. Religion often seems to be a box for our days of worship and our personal values, ethics and spiritual practices. Politics on issues like peace and the environment is in another box. Ken and I were both surprised to see each other that day in the 1990s, but Ken's *God Is Just Love* shows we shouldn't have been surprised.

Peace and the environment are two major life-shaping concerns for both Ken and me. As a high school student, I participated in the first Earth Day back in 1970. A friend and I organized a student environmental action group, and the first protest I participated in was one I planned as the school year came to a close. I went on to have a career as a religious peacemaker, travelling the world to teach conflict transformation. Sometimes the conflicts I entered had environmental centers, such as working with Indonesians struggling against the burning of the forests to make palm oil plantations. In September 2019 my wife Sharon and I were working and touring in England when the Global Climate Strike took place. After seeing the changing of the horse guards, we joined the march at the Houses of Parliament to support young people in the call for global action about climate change. In this context, Ken and I reconnected, bringing our relationship full circle as people of faith involved in the passionate work of resiliency for our planet in the face of dire threats.

We know we are not alone.

In this book Ken tells many stories of his children and provides resources for supporting and equipping our children and grandchildren as they face a grim future. He writes about—and with—hope. He often takes the lead from the children and their wisdom. Sharon and I involved our children in our peace and environmental work. I'll never forget taking preschooler Chris to a demonstration about the wars in Central America. As I was trying to explain to him why we were going and that we were trying to convince President Reagan to change his policies, Chris asked if we could pray for President Reagan. He stopped right there on the sidewalk and poured our his young passionate heart for the president to stop the wars.

Our son Jon in his early elementary years drew a picture of a stealth bomber. As he showed me his drawing with pride, I praised him on how well he had done and on the cool shape of the aircraft. Then I told him that the purpose of the bomber was to kill people. He ran off to his room. Soon he came back with another drawing of the bomber, this time with shirts, pants, hamburgers and fruit raining down from the bomber. He titled it "The Helping Stealth." Involving children in our work to heal the world allows them to become thoughtful agents even at a young age. They don't need to be passive but can begin to act now, with the discussions of caring adults willing to let them encounter tough issues in a context of love and hope. Ken's book is a gift to every family that wants to step boldly into a challenging future.

As a Christian faith leader, I am delighted to learn from the work Ken has done to integrate sincere religious faith with the vast wonders of science. Physics and astronomy have been academic hobbies of mine from an early age. What I have learned from the sciences hasn't threatened my faith but deepened my wonder and praise of the Creator and Sustainer of our astonishing cosmos. However, faith and science have also been viewed as opposing worldviews by some in both communities.

In extensive dialog with scientists and theologians, Ken shows the delightful and enriching complementarity of faith and science. Both can feed us mentally and emotionally, and both are needed to move us in constructive and creative ways in the face of the global perils we face.

Ken takes us back to the beginning with a fresh look at the biblical stories in Genesis. From the faith lessons learned and with the knowledge we gain from science Ken points the way forward with many practical ideas for personal and family engagement. If God is Just Love, as Ken states so clearly again and again, then we may find the hope we need to energize us for the tasks before us.

Daniel Buttry is a pastor, author, educator and peace activist who describes himself as a "peace warrior." He served for years as the Global Consultant for Peace and Justice with International Ministries of the American Baptist Churches. He is the author of many books about peacemaking, including Blessed Are the Peacemakers, a collection of profiles of peacemakers around the world.

Dear Readers,

Within this book are many gifts.

Some are for you as an adult. You will learn of parallels between truth as known by spirituality and science that are helpful as you try to understand and respond to the precarious state of our planet today. You will be asked to think about both your relationships and your ethics. You will find stories that will inspire, ideas that will make you smile and an overall message of hope, even in the midst of these perilous times.

Most of the gifts in this book are meant to be opened and shared with the children you care for, teach and treasure. You might enjoy reading them a story recommended in this book, perhaps again and again, about the creation and the stars. You might share the experience of wonderment with them, gazing towards the heavens on a starry night.

As you gaze into the heavens with a child, you might hear her calling out to you: "I am made of stardust."

"You certainly are a star," you might whisper back. In this way, love and truth are shared—and memories are built.

Only together can we hope to prepare our children to find hope and to be love, no matter what is happening in the world.

As you read this book, lights will come on to illuminate any darkness. You will discover answers to the question, "What matters most?"

Among them:

"Just Love"—and becoming this love.

Hope, and finding hope that is always sufficient.

Truth, and seeing reality that was hiding in plain sight.

In these pages, I am inviting you to travel alongside me and my family as we learn, grow and strive to choose rightly, adapt and care for the creation and each other, right now. Together we can grow the resilience, insights and skills needed in any future.

We are in this together.

Since I sent the author's draft of this book to the publisher in early February 2020, the circumstances of our lives have been changing more rapidly than anyone could have envisioned. It may even seem to you that the ways of life and the systems you counted on for happiness, and even survival, are being threatened. Will you have a job tomorrow? Can the government, businesses and other systems be counted on to provide for us and protect us? Will we ever return to normal? Not quickly. Not easily. The current health crisis is tragically connected to the global economic crisis. Both are exposing the reality of massive injustices in our world. Meanwhile, more wildfires are burning. More artic ice is melting.

All along, you have been doing everything you can think of to adapt, to support the children who need your reassurance and to care for friends and neighbors. As perils continue, though, we ask with more urgency: How do we stay healthy and, at the same time, connected to the people who sustain our lives? To the spiritual communities that nurture our souls?

Here is good news: The central message of this book is that we can find hope and "be love." We can build communities that allow us to live the core values that make life worth living, even as the times are radically changing.

How about decreasing consumption while increasing caring and sharing? How about celebrating diversity? We are in fact one. Everything is connected. At any moment, you and I can begin acting as one.

At the end of this book you will find a very diverse list entitled, *100 Things Families Can Do to Find Hope and Be Love*. I love this list! As I began compiling the list, I found myself starting to think of ideas, faster than I could write them down. I also loved it when I began sharing the list with friends, like my editor and his family, who immediately began generating ideas to add to the list. We are sharing this list with you because we are sure that one of the gifts of this book is encouragement to begin your own list of hopeful, loving ways we can make a difference each day.

As you read this book, you yourself are going to become an expert at deciding what you can and must do first, second and next.

Quite likely, this book's message of Just Love will inspire you. Your brain will spin with possibilities. Creativity and imagination will fill you and lift you up. You will use your precious life energy for being love, instead of wasting it on frantic consumption and fear.

Blessings flow when we honestly open our eyes, our minds and our spirits to the challenges of our world. In the New Testament of the Christian Bible, Jesus talks about the narrow path that leads towards abundant life. Western industrial civilization long ago took us far from that path. Now we must find our way back—back to the road that leads us through all valleys of shadows, beyond fear, towards joy, towards hope and love.

Finally, a word to readers who might shy away from a book that takes it as a given that our children will encounter grave difficulties in the days ahead. I want to assure you that you will not read gruesome descriptions of doom meant to guilt you towards some kind of action. I long ago abandoned scare tactics in my teaching. That does not work and is not the way of Just Love.

In these pages, you will find invitations to begin a conversation with me—and with all the people in your life who love their children the way you love yours. These conversations will lead us towards community. That community will lead us towards the love we need to live well—whatever the future holds.

We and our children have been given this world, and no other, by God. This time, and no other. We can choose to receive, open and use these gifts to serve the future of the children we love and all of God's creation.

Reading this book and living into its message may become the most exciting, meaningful and loving work you have ever undertaken. You will realize that you need help along the way.

That is my message: I can't do it alone. You can't do it alone.

But, we can do it together.

I can promise you that on this journey the love for your children will become, day by day, a more precious gift. You will plan exuberantly good times with them. Hope, you will learn, does not depend on every event working out as you planned. For you and your children, hope will become an action verb. You will experience and you will be love. You will be changed. You will endure. So will the children you love.

So, come along and meet my children and their children within the pages of this book.

Join us on this journey. On its own, this book is not enough.

This book needs you.

Looking forward,
Ken Whitt
Hide-A-Way Hills, Ohio
July 2020

The Children's Story

Jesus called a child, whom he put among them, and said,
"Truly I tell you, unless you change and become like children,
you will never enter the kingdom of heaven."
Matthew 18:2-3

Micah: Daddy, how much do you love me?
Daddy: As much as the sky. And how much does God love Micah?
Micah: As much as the stars.
Daddy: And how much does Micah love Daddy?
Micah: More than the sky.
Daddy: And how much does Micah love God?
Micah: (He looks puzzled.) Daddy, what is more than the stars?
Daddy: Well, the universe has zillions of them.
Micah: Then, more than everything.

My son, Micah, was 3 when I wrote down this conversation, but I had completely forgotten the writing and had only a dim memory of the event. Micah and I spoke of such things many times; ditto for his two sisters. The Daddy-Micah conversation had all the feeling of a sacrament whose origin was a couple of children's books that featured owls and rabbits. In fact, the dialog had become a common bedtime ritual. The love of which Micah spoke flowed into him and out from him. His parents taught him how to love and learned to love while caring for him. Micah knew love and was love. He was born that way.

Lauren, Micah's older sister, also was born that way. Even before her birth Lauren knew, and continues to know, "God loves me. I love God. Love in. Love out. Just like breathing." She was especially gifted at being tuned in to what everyone was feeling and what we needed. Lauren had herself participated many times in the "How much do I love you?" ritual. It was common for her to pop into conversations, like this:

> Micah: Daddy, where is God?
> Daddy: God is ...
> Lauren: God is in the flowers and the trees. That is why they are so beautiful.
> Micah: You're beautiful.
> Lauren: That's because God is inside me, and inside you. God is also inside the animals.

Stacey, age 8 at this time, was the beloved leader of our gang of three. She also had a way of showing up, almost on cue. Lauren's word about God in the animals was an opportunity not to be missed. She strode into Micah's room and questioned:

> Stacey: Daddy, if God is in the animals, then why can't we have a puppy?
> Daddy: How about some fish?
> Stacey: Daddy, you know what happened the last time our fish had babies.
> Daddy: Shh! Don't remind your sister. That still makes her sad.

Stacey had a way of taking our conversations about God and love a bit too literally.

> Daddy: God is everywhere. God is inside you.
> Stacey: (Examines her hand.) Like my blood and my bones.
> Daddy: Not quite. God is love. You can feel love and you can give love, but you cannot see love. God is just like that. When you are happy and loving, Stacey—you too, Micah and Lauren—I can see God's love in your smile and in your kindness. You are the best big sister!
> Stacey: So, if I keep being kind, what about the puppy?

How did I finally remember this long-forgotten conversation? About a week before I began writing this chapter, Kathy and I were in the final weeks of packing up our house for our move back to Ohio, where all the children live with their children. We were downsizing our lives and sorting every single thing—as many items as the stars in the sky— keeping this, giving that away. This goes in the garbage. I can't decide about that. You know the routine.

In a closet, on the shelves of a bookcase, there had been stacks of a couple thousand sermon manuscripts dating back to the 1970s. I couldn't just heave them all! Beginning six months earlier, I had been examining each one, keeping the best. On Saturday, March 2, 2019, I spied the final stack of about 100 unsorted sermons from my last two years as pastor of the First Baptist Church of Littleton, Massachusetts, 1988-89. I was so sick of sorting and packing that I wanted to dump them all in the paper recycling box under my desk. But I paused, hesitated, looked down. On top of the pile was a message titled, "The Cosmic Scope of the Christian Venture." I was astounded. The sermon, dated February 19, 1989, bore an uncanny resemblance to some of the primary insights of my current research and writing project on spirituality and science.

Hastily, I set aside the remaining 99 and sat down to read the nearly abandoned sermon. That was where I found, not only the conversation with my young children, but also a reminder of some of the ways we as parents had sought to nurture the love that is the birthright of Stacey, Lauren, Micah, Sally and all the children of the world. I slipped that document into a folder to show my now very grown-up children on our next visit, the following Tuesday.

I knew that sharing the sermon with my children was going to be a pleasant upshot of this unexpected encounter with the past. At first, I had no idea that I was also encountering a significant God event. With "The Cosmic Scope of the Christian Venture" tucked into a folder in my briefcase, the first stop on our whirlwind trip of four days was a meeting with the founder and publisher of Read the Spirit Books. David Crumm and his editorial team had recently agreed to publish my book, *God Is Just Love*. We decided to meet face to face to begin our work together.

I handed David a draft of my book. He took a quick look at the opening lines of what was then Chapter 1 and firmly told me, "This opens too slowly. This won't work." Then he told me a story about gold coins. "Imagine, Ken, that you and your wife are hiking in the mountains and have found a beautiful meadow full of flowers and the songs of birds. You are resting on a log, when Kathy spots what looks like the entrance of a trail into an unfamiliar and shadowy forest. You walk toward that forest and stand at the trail's beginning. There is a hint of rain in the air. You are not sure you have time to explore a new trail. Besides, Kathy thinks it looks a bit ominous. You're just about to head back down the mountain, when she spots a glitter of light just a few yards down the trail. She steps into the forest to check it out and finds a gold coin. You both laugh over your good fortune. Then, you see another flash. And another glitter. And another flash. Soon you are deep into the forest—on an adventure.

"Good books are like that," David said. "Your first chapter has to offer a gold coin that will invite your readers to turn the page in search of the next gold coin. Soon, they have eagerly joined you in this adventure."

I beamed with excitement. "I've got one, right here—a story from 30 years ago that I was going to share with my children tomorrow."

David read the dialog between Stacey, Lauren, Micah and their daddy, and pronounced, "This is the beginning of the first chapter. It's a remarkable story you have just rediscovered in your own life." I got the point, but not the whole point. That only came later when, over the next few days, I had surprisingly deep and expansive conversations with each of my children—exactly as David advised me to do. Within those conversations we all remembered more of the gold coins of our family's adventures through life together.

The four conversations with my children and their spouses were all energetic and revealing. Each covered the same three topics, but with a distinctive focus. The three topics were:

1. The experience and celebration of love in our family.
2. The encounters with the creation that opened all of us to awe and wonder.
3. The exposure to all kinds of diversity that taught us to care about everything and everyone.

I asked questions and listened as my children opened their memories and their hearts. As they spoke, I continued to remember how intentional we had been as parents in passing on core values. I began to notice how these core values are related to the shared truth known by spirituality and science. Let me amplify those values:

1. **Love**—Science and spirituality together know that something awesome and mysterious is holding the universe together and propelling creation forward. We are all connected and inextricably bound together. Science uses the term "fields" to describe various forms of this force. "In Christ," we know this force as love.

2. **Wonderment**—Science and spirituality together know that the universe is glorious. Mysterious. Both known and unknown. Black holes have been "seen." A near infinite diversity of wonders is available to those who see the Earth in its majesty. "In Christ," we give God the glory and know God's presence in the whole shebang.

3. **Diversity**—Everything and everyone has intrinsic value that is not dependent on their usefulness to human beings. Science and spirituality together know that everything and everyone is connected; we are one. The well-being of one is the well-being of all, and that includes the entire creation. "We are one in the Spirit, we are one in the Lord."

Families have the primary responsibility for teaching and living these values. Are these the core values of families in our culture, and our country as a whole?

I observed a modern family today. This was not an everyday sight for me, so I took notice and immediately thought, "How cute!" I was getting my car serviced. There was this hipster father and his daughter and son. My car dealer is tech friendly. The family of three was seated at one of those state-of-the-art high-rise tables with outlets and USB ports for computers and other devices. Dad, daughter, about age 10, and son, about age 3, were all plugged in. Dad was dressed in Nike head to toe, with black earphones. Son's earphones were blue and the daughter's earphones were pink. I also noticed, when it was time for them to pick up their car and leave, that they exited in a solemn, silent procession, each still tuned to signals in the air.

I don't recall any feeling of judgment, at the time. However, that evening I was typing the transcript of a two-hour interview conducted with my son, Micah, and his wife, Jen. Toward the end of the interview, I was anxious when I needed to ask a difficult question that could be painful to answer.

Ken: *Micah, Jen, I must ask this question. What do you fear about the world your children are growing up in?*

Jen: *My biggest fear for Audrey is the consuming nature and disconnecting nature of technology. I think that in our generation we had a childhood without technology. Technology didn't descend on us until after we had grown up in a world of imagination. A lot of my generation are addicted to technology, but we still remember and can return to the other side ...*

Micah: *We are the last generation ...*

Jen: *Our kids will never know a world without overwhelming technology. I want our kids to know how to use technology as a tool but to see the world way beyond that. I am so nervous about how to teach that. Literally, kids are addicted to it. It's like a drug that pulls them away from nature, from imagination, from play, from creativity. It really scares me. We must have phones and computers and our kids have to learn their way around this technology. I think the only way to combat this addiction is to make sure there is much more about life that is enjoyable. Technology will be there, but make sure it is not a super magnet. We are doing a great job with Audrey as a 2-year-old, but how do we continue this? Right now, we make it a big deal that watching a show is a special event. When it's over Audrey happily heads toward something else. How do we continue this as she gets older?*

Micah: I really try, whenever possible, to encourage Audrey
to play with things that are tactile, things she puts
together or builds. We can't escape entirely the lights
and sounds of technology, but as much as possible we
can, often by playing with her, teach her to enjoy and
develop skills, creating a city with blocks, organizing
a farm with animals, and figuring out how things
work. By taking the time with Audrey we can help her
grow her interest in reading books more and looking
at screens much less.

Jen: You have asked us to reflect on the purpose of our lives:
I know that God is teaching me through my vocation.
That really matters. But what matters more is what I
am doing as a parent; and you have to know, many
parents are not parenting. They are getting by ...

Micah: They are surviving ...

Jen: They don't have the time or energy or longing to be
intentional. Micah and I take this role seriously and
spend a lot of time talking about our role as parents.
Our calling now is to craft these little human beings
into vessels of love for God. It's really an honor. It's
really a cool job. I feel so grateful that I get to do this,
and we get to do this together and God is continuing to work through us and provide us what we need.
That's my purpose now.

Micah: We don't know what the world will be like. What we
can do is decide what core values will be best for our
children and for the world. We can make sure they get
to know all kinds of people and that they learn to treat
people well. They can learn to fight for causes that
make the world a better place, fight for justice reform
in a lot of different areas, environment, prison reform.
We can teach our kids to question what they learn in
school. What's in the books may not be all there is to
it. That's a big lesson as they get older, especially when

it comes to history, to be able to question and look for injustice.

What's at stake is the capacity of our children to thrive and know love and be love and do justice and make peace, no matter what is going on around them. One of Jen's and Micah's deep longings is to introduce their children to a planet's worth of diversity and wonder, to know many different people and to see many different places. That is how their children will learn that everything is connected and everyone and everything is part of God's good creation. But, of course, they don't have all the time and money in the world to accomplish this parenting goal. At one point in the conversation I jumped in and declared:

Ken: *Do you have any idea how much I want to help you to do that? I have limits too, like my aging body, but I also have some time and some money to help you—especially as your kids get older—to share the world with your children. You know how Makenna (a 6-year-old cousin) loves science!? Just recently, she and I took in two shows at the planetarium and I have been teaching her how to use star-gazing binoculars—and we bought her a telescope for Christmas.*

My wife, Kathy, and I are always looking for opportunities. One day after we moved to Ohio, she came home excited about a friend's recommendation of a new John Glenn Astronomy Park in the Hocking Hills State Park. I immediately Googled the park, learned a few things and then passed that news on to our family, planting another seed that might help expand our children's awareness of the world. Opportunities abound to reconnect our children to the creation, to wonderment.

I also found it intriguing that in the minds of the next generation, concern for the impact of technology was connected to planetary issues like eco-justice. I raised that issue with a friend, the Rev. Michael Dowd, author of *Thank God for Evolution* and a leading authority on eco-justice. My question to Michael was:

Ken: *Does this issue of our addiction to technology in some*
way relate to our concerns about the fate of the Earth
and preparing our children for whatever comes?
Michael: *First of all. I am eternally grateful that Alison and*
I shared a largely common worldview in our mar-
riage. We shared an understanding that technology is
not morally neutral. Technology helps human beings
but harms virtually everything else. In the begin-
ning, of course, there was God's technology, that is
nature's technology. Everything lives, then dies and
becomes food for another life form. Human technol-
ogies die and become garbage that cannot integrate
into nature's technology. We become more and more
self-centered, human-centered. It is all about us and
to hell with the rest of the creation. With our children,
Alison and I tried to instill caring for everything and
everyone. That value in itself is anti-technology.

When we were parenting our young children, back in the 1980s, Michael and I were both pastors of small Baptist churches in Massachusetts. Our families were friends and shared many good times. We spent a vacation week together in the Catskill Mountain region of upstate New York. Swimming. Fishing. Canoeing. Creeking. S'moreing. Hiking. Exploring. Stargazing in the meadow late into the night.

Our families were living the same core values. Our children now have grown and are passing these values to their children: Love. Wonderment. Diversity.

I believe millions of families all over the world are trying to prepare the children we love to find hope—and to be love—no matter the perils we encounter. No matter what comes next.

2

The Seeing Tree

Zacchaeus was a wee little man,
A wee little man was he.
He climbed up in a sycamore tree,
For he wanted his Lord to see.
(a popular children's song)

Once upon a time I was called to preach at a church that was anything but loving. The spirit of that church was, "division." The testimony of the church was "love," but this was a concept, not a practice; words, not deeds. Their desire to be loving seemed to be tied up in knots, tied tight by exclusion. Knowing that, I prepared for them a sermon entitled, "The Seeing Tree." It was a message about Jesus and his ever-so-short friend Zacchaeus. The crowd was so big and the men and women were so tall that he had to climb a sycamore tree to see Jesus.

I also wrote a song with the same title:

Zacchaeus climbed a seeing tree, and what he saw was Jesus.
Zacchaeus climbed a seeing tree, and what he saw was life.
Zacchaeus climbed a seeing tree, and what he found was pardon,
Zacchaeus climbed a seeing tree, and what he found was love.

It was a pretty good song and a great message. The problem was that I was only passing through. What would I leave behind that could be a reminder that God Is Just Love? That is when I began inventing my own physical symbol of A Seeing Tree. This seeing tree also began as a sycamore tree growing on our land in the Catskill Mountains. I had already cut one of the smaller ones down in order to turn it into lumber. From one of its branches I cut dozens of slices. Many eventually morphed into bases for seeing trees called Trinity Candles.

The Trinity Candles, as I began building them, include four LED lights. The yellow one in the middle is you and me. The three candles surrounding us are the Creator, the Christ and the Holy Spirit. I have made and given away dozens of Trinity Candles. My favorite ones have God candles that cycle through the colors red, orange, green and purple. These motion lights suggest that the word "God," is more like an action verb than a static noun. Love is always on the move, accomplishing the purposes of God.

At the end of my sermon I gave the church a Trinity Candle and told them:

> *I made a gift for your church to help you remember that you can always see Jesus and be Jesus to others. This is a Trinity Candle. You, and everyone else, including people who are different or those you do not like, are in the center. You live and move and have your being inside the love of our Father, Son, Holy Spirit God. No one is left out. Everyone is loved unconditionally and eternally. If one is lost, are all lost. If one is excluded, all are left in the dark. "Love your neighbor as yourself," means that your neighbor is yourself. We are one in Christ. One in love. Remember, God is Just Love.*

The Gospel of John announces, "For God so loved the world ..."

A parable told by Jesus celebrates the love of a shepherd who left 99 sheep to go in search of one who was lost. Jesus also tells the story of a father with two very different sons that suggests God is a father who, without condition, welcomes home a child who had been disobedient, disgraceful and disgusting. We know from the Hebrew Scriptures that God loves as the prophet Hosea loved his incessantly unfaithful wife. God, like Hosea, is betrayed again and again. God keeps seeking and forgiving. It is said in the Quran (39:53, 25:63-76) that God pronounced, "My servants who have harmed yourselves by your own excess, do not despair of God's mercy. God forgives all sins. God is truly the most forgiving, the most merciful."

Still, protests abound from the spiritually blind. Those of us who already have claimed our full measure of mercy, grace and love murmur against God's eternal mercy. We condemn another judged to be a more terrible sinner. Some of us even imagine that we know, based on some authority like tradition, where the moral line is to be drawn, one sin being categorically more immoral, and thus sufficient ground for exclusion, than another.

Shall I, with my unmeasured fury, launch a protest movement against God's mercy, like the one launched by the elder brother against the father who welcomed home his lost son? (Luke 5:15) Are there some of us who, considering our sins quite minor, would set up our pile of stones to pummel a woman caught in adultery? (John 8:4) As the owner of a flock of 100 sheep, would I fire the shepherd for irresponsible abandonment of the 99 sheep? (Luke 15:4) Some among us are intolerant of a tolerant God; some representatives of religion cannot abide a God of Just Love. So, we complicate the matter and lay intolerable burdens upon the souls of children of God who can only be saved by believing in Just Love.

Clearly, the phrase "Just Love" has multiple meanings. First, it means "only love." Simply put, as in the New Testament letter of 1 John, God is love. Love is God. The testimony of uncounted spiritual masters throughout human history, and from all the world's great spiritual traditions, tells me this is true. However, the authority of all of these witnesses is insufficient to convince the deep down inside of me that this is true. My experience, my relationship with God, is what leads to my certainty.

A friend asked me, "What if my experience of God is different? What if God has been for me just angry, or just absent?"

I did not answer quickly. Her question was also her experience. Her answer had caused her deep suffering. But finally, I had to speak the truth I had learned over 40 years of pastoral ministry among thousands of people. I spoke from my heart to hers: "My long experience with many people has convinced me that a prerequisite of a whole and abundant life is the experience of unconditional love. To any person whose deep experience is of a judgmental and angry god, I must give the counsel, "Your image of God must change."

"What does that mean?" she protested. "How do I do that?"

My attempt at a loving response only elicited confusion from my friend. But our conversation did not end that day. We have continued sharing, listening and reflecting. Now and then she will share with me a thought, or even an experience, of Presence that seems to be, not angry; rather, protective, caring. Images of God often change slowly and are grounded in new life experiences of love, coming from somewhere, and the willingness to consider the possibility that that "somewhere" is God.

Most of us are glad to know that we are not puppets on a string, manipulated by the fingers of feckless fate. The flip side of the gift of freedom is that the God of Just Love respects that freedom and waits for us to "knock at the door." God loves us and is seeking us. However, we do have to knock with words, prayers and actions. You can begin to take steps forward, kind of like an experiment, that give God an opportunity to show up in your world. Do something different, like walking in the woods, reading a devotional book, asking a friend for help or watching a movie with a spiritual message. Of course, there is also the way that many addicts have told me worked for them. You wait until you hit rock bottom, are about to die, and some long buried desperate hope within you cries out for help. This—a baseball bat smashed against your head—is a very dangerous path. There are many paths but all of them require surrender. And surrender nearly always feels like jumping off a cliff.

Thousands of witnesses, millions of stories, but especially my own story, convince me that nothing could possibly matter more than the belief, the experience, of God being Just Love.

Second, the phrase "Just Love" helps us to grasp the mystery that "love," as understood by human beings, is insufficient to define the full truth of God as Love. In the Bible, the words "justice" and "love" occur often in close proximity to each other. The attentive reader is hard pressed to escape the conclusion that the two words are pointing towards the same reality. Are other words and images and stories and metaphors, besides "just," also needed to help human beings approach the full meaning of the image of God as Just Love? Of course. And we have millions of such stories and metaphors at our disposal; and like the expanding universe, the number of such stories is ever-growing towards infinity. Just read Scripture, from all traditions. Or ask me, or millions of others, to tell you my latest God story. Or ask, for example, author and Christian believer

Ted Dekker to tell you a story about Jesus. Read his books, *A.D. 30* and *A.D. 33*, and prepare yourself to experience the Way of Jesus as you never have. Be ready to experience Just Love through a story. The Christian Scriptures, all the Scriptures of the world's spiritual traditions, tell compelling stories that are like a bridge from despair to hope, emptiness to fullness, fear to faith.

We also can learn this lesson from our Jewish friends. At the High Holidays each year, Jews gather during the Yom Kippur day of fasting and repentance, trusting in God's love and compassion. One translation of a prayer for Yom Kippur reflects the Jewish faith that God will always be merciful—as if God's own response to our human failings will be:

> *May it be My will that My mercy suppress my anger, and that it prevail over My attributes of justice and judgment; and that I may deal with My children according to the attribute of compassion, and that I may not deal with them according to the strict line of justice.*

This prayer envisioned by Jewish sages suggests that perhaps it is difficult, painful and risky for God to be Just Love. I am convinced that God suffers as God loves. I am convinced, as illuminated by my experience as a parent, that Just Love makes God vulnerable. This vulnerability is included, in fact is a necessary part of, Just Love. God as love does not have total control. The beloved, by definition—this is the inviolate nature of love—has the power of choice. Wrong choices result in terrible consequences. Evil takes root. Still, God is Just Love. You can see this love in operation when the worst mistake a person has ever made has the ironic consequence of offering up an opportunity to make the next best, lifesaving and love-affirming choice.

The metaphor, "God Is Just Love," is not the complete story concerning God. However, it is full of use. Full of wisdom. Full of truth. Full of benefits to all of us, the entire Earth community and the whole magnificent cosmos. Twelve-step programs tell their participants that their salvation from addiction depends on knowing a higher power. Call it God, call it friend, call it tree—you don't have to get it all right to get it to work for you! Knowing God is all about relating to God, not thinking about God. Allow God as Just Love to be the center of your life. Say "yes," to God and an abundant life is yours—not an easy or safe life but a blessed life. You become the love you know. You become Just Love for others, for the world.

Here is one of the many places that science and spirituality converge: Both explore the unknown because they believe that knowing the truth matters immensely. But you don't have to know everything for what you do know to be valuable. At least for the time being, scientists have to be content with knowledge that falls short of a theory of everything. The current wisdom is that the universe burst forth from what they call a "singularity." Scientists know a lot about that beginning of the universe and most likely will learn a lot more. But where did that singularity, often called the "one source," come from and what was inside it? I believe that there is compelling evidence that, from the beginning of time and space, beauty, purpose and desire, longing, consciousness have been the essence of the force that brought all things into being and holds all things together. There is a wealth of experience confirming the presence of these imponderables in our universe. They are as real as anything science confirms through observations and experiments.

For example, there are an overwhelming number of testimonies and many studies, that confirm the belief that love heals—and that faith promotes health. Many "blue zones," scattered around the world, are religious communities. Within these zones people live healthier and longer lives. Even the scientists of the World Health Organization are carefully examining the factors present in religious communities that promote abundant life.

The presence of awe-inspiring beauty dazzles and mystifies scientists as much as the rest of us. The appearance of intelligence and conscious-ness suggest to many scientists that these qualities of life were present as potentials from the beginning—somehow the universe knew we were coming. Everything that exists in the universe has its origin in energy. Love is energy. Love is always in motion. Love is always happening, unfolding. How about we unfold with it, becoming love?

The Force Is the Source on Course

At the beginning of my two years of focused study and writing on spirituality and science, the sciences that I studied most eagerly were physics, quantum mechanics and astrophysics. As an excitable beginner, I saw consistency between spirituality and science everywhere. I was like a sponge, soaking up everybody else's conclusions as to how their spiritual ideas were confirmed by science and supported science. Fortunately, there were a few scientists and others in my world who steered me towards the most reputable scholars of both science and religion. I ingested books and asked questions and frequently changed my mind. New information, from both spirituality and science, always has to be considered. But eventually conclusions can be shared.

After much consideration, one of the main conclusions from my research has a ring that *Star Wars* fans will appreciate: **The Force is the Source on Course.**

Here is what I mean in three steps:

1. **Singularity** (one source) = **Love** (the Word)

From the point of view of science, the source is the singularity filled to overflowing with one ancestral force—energy and possibilities about to become a universe.

From the point of view of Christ-centered spirituality, the source is the energy of the Pure Spirit of Love, the Word that God has just spoken, about to become a universe.

2. **Force = Christ**

From the point of view of science, the force is energy that speeds forth from the singularity to make a universe. There are both "ever expanding forces" and "ever binding together forces," in just the right balance so that the universe can both expand and stick together.

From the point of view of Christianity, the *force* is Christ, the One who brings all things into being and holds all things together; in just the right balance so that the universe can both expand and stick together.

3. **Course** (all the possibilities) = **Creation** (everything unfolding according to the purposes of love)

From the point of view of science, the course included, from the beginning, all the possibilities that might be birthed; everything that was and was to be was already present in the singularity. The theory known as "the weak anthropic cosmological principle," is a name scientists give to the presence at the beginning of all that the universe would become.

From the point of view of Christianity, the course is the creation unfolding from the beginning in the direction of God's eternal purpose, which is love. Christians sing, "As it was in the beginning, is now and ever shall be, world without end, amen, amen."

Please note that in the above paragraphs, the emphasis is on potential, possibilities, rather than a pre-determined plan. Think about the difference in meaning of the words "determined" and "possibilities." The weak anthropic cosmological principle, a theory that emerges out of quantum physics, affirms that in the beginning, within the singularity, there was already present all the potential and possibility that we now know as the reality of our universe. Possibilities, not a plan. Unpredictability, not certainty. Freedom, not control.

I am a spiritual seeker and a student of science committed to pursuing truth. Words like "possibilities," "uncertainty" and "lack of control" say a lot about my experience of life, including everything about loving my children. I saw within my children possibilities that I could encourage and support, but no plan I could control. I loved my children and so I set them free, experiencing again how vulnerable we are as parents.

Kahil Gibran, Christian mystic, writer, poet says this about children to their parents:

> *Your children are not your children.*
> *They are the sons and daughters of life longing for itself.*
> *They come through you but not from you*
> *And though they are with you, they belong not to you.*
> *You can give them your love but not your thoughts,*
> *For they have their own thoughts.*
> *You may house their bodies, but not their souls,*
> *For their souls dwell in the house of tomorrow,*
> *Which you cannot visit, not even in your dreams.*

(from The Prophet, "On Children")

God is often thought of as a loving parent. Is God also limited in God's ability to control the decisions we will make? In extending love to creation and creatures, is God vulnerable to suffering as human mothers and fathers are? Are uncertainty—and the possibility of disappointment and pain—inherent in the meaning of Just Love, even for God?

I think so. I experience it as so. I believe the Bible tells me so. As I have proposed in "The Force is the Source on Course," I believe that all we know as "reality" sprang from the love of God going forth in Christ to make a world. No scientist can say, as a scientist, that the singularity, the one source, was Just Love. But many scientists, as persons of faith, do come to spiritual conclusions very much like that.

Anyone who studies the scientific creation story winds up in awe of the miniscule odds against our universe hanging together without flying apart or collapsing in on itself. Experts who examine the mathematical analysis of this process can be as dumbstruck as a lovestruck teenager. The beauty and diversity and complexity of life, and the inexplicable advent of consciousness, can point them as spiritual seekers towards Just Love. And Just Love can then motivate everything that a scientist does with everything they know.

Recently I was having a spiritual conversation with a scientist about our unique experiences of God. Willow DiLuzio, Ph.D, a Harvard graduate in chemical engineering, talked with me about her vocation:

> *In choosing my field of study and eventually accepting a job offer, I knew that God was guiding me. Before graduation everyone was sending out resumes. I sent out a lot. Back then I was a lot closer to God than I have been in recent years; the church in Littleton was part of my family. My memories of our mission trip to Arizona were sharp and I had been receiving a lot of support from my friends there, through all the difficult times, you know ... A lot of chemical engineers go to work in chemical plants and oil refineries, but I knew that was not what I wanted to do. My training also was good for a lot of pharmaceutical companies, and I started out working in a lab.*
>
> *My work has always been developing new drugs. I know that pharmaceutical companies have a really bad rap. But people*

who take their training and choose to work at pharmaceutical companies find the main goal is to cure disease—it really is. Really good people go to work there because they want to make a difference in people's lives. Literally, for me, it was, on the one hand, make oil, on the other hand, make life saving drugs. Those were my main choices.

The projects I have worked on have really helped people. For my second job, seven years, the whole time we were working on improving medications for ulcerative colitis and Crohn's disease. It is not a fatal disease, but I know people who have it, and it really impacts their lives. People can't leave their homes. That's the product I worked on most. It's approved now and we just filed for a new version that will be like an injector pen that people can take home and treat themselves. Hopefully that will be approved soon.

In the end, I know that I have helped people have better lives. So often I have had to explain to my daughter, Jasmine, that I had to go on a work trip. Yes, I would miss something important in the family. But I told her, God gave me this opportunity and the skill to really help others. I make medicines so that people can be healthy and happy. It's about just loving people—a lot of people. If I didn't do it, I would be wasting the gift God gave me. That is how I have explained it to her, as a child, but I really believe this. If I have the skills, I have a responsibility to use them well for a better world.

The new company I am looking at is working on gene therapy. Gene therapy has the potential to cure people. They get one treatment and it fixes DNA and you are cured forever. There are a lot of clinical trials going on, especially for rare childhood diseases. The company I am looking at is working on muscular dystrophy. Kids with muscular dystrophy have been dying before 20—but now there is an approved product and kids are living beyond 20. This has never been seen before! So, it's an

exciting vocation. Big medical breakthroughs, and I have a
chance to be a part of that.

There are many scientists, Willow DiLuzio among them, who are motivated by Just Love, guided in their daily lives and work by that love, and who are filled with gratitude for the opportunities they are given to be love to others.

Love is working its way through the universe and has been doing so since the beginning. Love is working its way into our lives and out from our lives.

Though we often wish it were not so, love also works its way towards completion through the experience of death. Sorry, there is no way of avoiding this facet of love's work. We live. We die. Life is followed by death and then, throughout the entirety of creation, resurrection follows death. Just Love is working its way across the universe and through our lives, even within the tragedy and suffering that are inevitable in even the most loving and abundant life. Knowing this, believing this deeply enough so that trust in God can put down the deepest roots in the ground of my life, has for me required both knowledge of science and spirituality.

I was astounded by a story I heard a couple of years ago while attending a program sponsored by the Spiritual Renewal Center in Syracuse, New York. The presenter was George Coyne, Ph.D, a Jesuit scholar and formerly the director of the Vatican Observatory. Destruction, he told us, is at the heart of the creative process in our universe. Life is impossible on this created world without destruction—including those events that we call catastrophes. Coyne explained that our sun is a third-generation star, formed 3 to 4 billion years ago, from the debris created by the explosion of a supernova. That cataclysmic event began when a second-generation star, which had been birthed from debris of a first-generation star, approached the end of its life. That star had about 4.5 billion birthdays, but finally it was that star's time to die! That star was formed from the materials available in the universe following the big bang, helium and hydrogen. The conditions present in the first supernova brought new elements into existence, but it is the second supernova that created the elemental building blocks of life, like carbon.

In John 12:24, Jesus tells us: "Very truly, I tell you, unless a grain of wheat falls into the earth and dies, it remains just a single grain; but if it dies, it bears much fruit."

I know, from experience, the testimony of Scripture, and from science, that resurrection—life arising from death—is the way of the universe, the way of life on the planet Earth and the deep spirituality of my life.

For everything there is a season, and a time for every matter under heaven:

> *a time to be born, and a time to die;*
> *a time to plant, and a time to pluck up what is planted;*
> *a time to kill, and a time to heal;*
> *a time to break down, and a time to build up;*
> *a time to weep, and a time to laugh;*
> *a time to mourn, and a time to dance;*

Ecclesiastes 3:1-4, NRSV

When we accept these truths, then we can trust in God, no matter the circumstances. You fight for life or you let go of life. Both, in their seasons, are what love requires. God is Just Love in both our living and in our dying.

When, from your own seeing tree, you see and believe, fear of death vanishes. From the vantage point of the Gospels, see Jesus and you are more than a conqueror, no matter the conflict. Being that Christ is everywhere and in everything, there is no tree or perch—no place or time, where Christ can not be seen with the eyes of faith.

Here's another verse of "The Seeing Tree," reminding us of the story of Jesus's mother, Mary.

> *Mary climbed a seeing tree; for the first time she saw Jesus,*
> *Mary's sorrow was her seeing tree, showing her the way to life,*
> *Grieving was her seeing tree, tears opened her to mercy,*
> *Emptiness was her seeing tree, healing her heart with love.*

What's your verse? Even now, your verse is being sung in the heart of God. Hear the song. Find the hope. Be the love.

3

Time and the Kingdom of God

*Jesus came to Galilee, proclaiming the good news of God, and
saying, "The time is fulfilled, and the kingdom of God has
come near; repent, and believe in the good news."*
Mark 1:14b-15, NRSV

Truth, whether approached through science or spirit, ultimately is one. Accompanied by an open mind, heart and spirit, many who are earnestly seeking truth are finding diverse points of convergence between spirituality and science. Knowing and living the truth sets us free to live well, whatever the circumstances that confront us.

Have you ever been told that a spiritual idea can't be true because it is not logical? Many spiritual principles, and many discoveries of science, are true even though they defy common sense. Their truth lies beyond human logic. Read the Beatitudes of Jesus from the Gospel of Matthew (Matthew 5:1-12). Back in the 1980s there was a season of my life when the leading of the Spirit seemed to be telling me to dive into the deep sea of my suffering. A voice of wisdom kept telling me, "Don't dodge it; swim in it. And, I will be with you." While that may not seem logical—those of us who have lived through a dark night of the soul will tell you that such experiences also open doors to transformation. Sometimes, our best days follow.

I realize that, in this book, I am asking you to consider some impossible possibilities. So, let's explore one of these impossibilities, our understanding of time itself. Think of this as one of the rabbit holes that leads to Alice's wonderland. It's also a great illustration of the way science and spirituality converge on non-rational truth.

What Is Time?

Human beings think that we understand time. Nothing could be further from the truth. As a human being, you will likely need to stretch your imagination to make sense of the following conversation, even though the insightful one is a child.

Remember the bedtime ritual described in Chapter 1?

Micah: Daddy, how much do you love me?
Daddy: As much as the sky. And how much does God love Micah?
Micah: As much as the stars.
Daddy: And how much does Micah love Daddy?
Micah: More than the sky.
Daddy: And how much does Micah love God?
Micah: (He looks puzzled.) Daddy, what is more than the stars?
Daddy: Well, the universe has zillions of them.
Micah: Then, more than everything.

Over the years, that ritual changed among my three children. There were additions and deletions. The questions and answers matured. But can you imagine a time when a child's wisdom seemed to pass out of time and head towards eternity?

Stacey: Daddy, how long has God been in love with me?
Daddy: Well, let me think. I think the only right answer has to be, "forever."
Stacey: But that does not make any sense.
Daddy: It doesn't? How so?
Stacey: God is Love before time begins. God is Love after time ends.
Daddy: So, how long has God's loved you?
Stacey: It has to be, Before Forever/Forever/After Forever.
Daddy: But isn't that the same as, "forever."
Stacey: Of course not, Daddy, just dream about it.

This is poetry, if I ever heard it, and I still have difficulty grasping it.

Years ago, Catholic mystic Thomas Merton, in his book, *Love and Living*, called for a "spiritual balance" that could help us make sense of reality; the world as it really is. Merton told us that we need to know the truth found at the convergence of contemplative and scientific disciplines. We need to become both poet and physicist, priest and psychologist, monk and politician. Without this balance, our end, Merton predicts, can only be "madness." From within the truth found at the points of convergence of spirituality and science, we learn the truth and become the sanity that will teach us how to ready our children to find hope and be love.

For that reason, I invite you to dive deep into this chapter. I also invite you, as the need may arise, to translate the Christian images and ideas you find into your own language of faith and love. So, I ask the question again. "What is time?" What do both science and spirituality tell us about time that we must know in order to find hope and be love?

Both scientists and spiritual seekers know something that popular opinion pretty much ignores. Physicists and mystics know that there is, in reality, no past, present or future—except for the subjective fact that human beings need to think of time that way. We can live our daily lives no other way. To deny experiences like preparing for the future, moving on, the march of time, and the necessity to not waste time would be to deny our humanity. Yet, if the mystics and physicists are correct, in some way our subjective experience is an illusion.

Let's look at a passage of Scripture from Genesis 6:6-7: "And the Lord was sorry that he had made humankind on the earth, and it grieved him to his heart. So, the Lord said, "I will blot out from the earth the human beings I have created—people together with animals and creeping things and birds of the air, for I am sorry that I have made them.""

For many years, I struggled mightily with this text because it seems to declare that God can change God's mind—that God's destructive anger can displace God's creative love. I had discussions, deep and difficult, with Jewish students of Torah, with whom I have often consulted. I wrestled with these texts.

Then I began applying the strange concept of time to the text. For the Genesis storyteller, the story must be told sequentially, one thing following another. The story progresses from point A to point B and so on through history. At point D, humanity may experience a revelation of God's character unknown before, but in the heart of God these revelations were all present at the beginning, all preexistent in the heart of God. They are eternally true. Love unfolds in the universe. Love expands and evolves in the creation. But love cannot stop being love. The essence of reality that brought all things into being and holds all things together does not become something different when reality, as experienced by humans, becomes difficult. What *is* is what was and what is to come. There are no moments in time when God changes the purpose behind creation. If both life and death are part of the fabric of creation, then love does not "give up" on love just because death is painful to us, or even to God.

Being Inside and Outside of Time—At the Same Time

With that background, we come to the crucial point of this chapter—two of the core themes in the ministry of Jesus:

1. The Kingdom of God
2. The imminent end of history and the urgency of our response

The Christian world is deeply divided on exactly what Jesus meant when he talked about The Kingdom of God and the imminent end of the age. This controversy has become particularly acute in our era because so many voices, mine included, are calling Christians to begin again to discern what it means to be a follower of Jesus. Radical change is afoot in the Christian world. Many of us are calling on Christians to get to know Jesus again, as if for the first time.

So, what was Jesus talking about when he referred to the Kingdom? In general, the Kingdom of God refers to the rule of God in history and in eternity; the rule of God in time and out of time; the rule of God in the hearts of all of God's children, among all the nations, yet especially within believers and the church. In the Gospel of Mark, the first written Gospel, the very first words of Jesus are: "The time is fulfilled, and the Kingdom of God has come near; repent and believe in the good news." (Mark 1:15)

Whatever Jesus may mean by the Kingdom of God, the Kingdom is at the core of his life and teaching. Yet, that teaching does seem neither logical nor consistent. Descriptions of the Kingdom include:

- The Kingdom is near; and the Kingdom is here.
- The Kingdom is coming; and the Kingdom has arrived.
- The Kingdom is within you; and the Kingdom is among you.
- Grasp the Kingdom right now; and be ready for the Kingdom when it comes.
- Don't miss the Kingdom; but don't be deceived by the announcement by others of its arrival.
- Everything is in God's hands; and we must grasp the Kingdom with our hands.

Jesus was trying to teach them, and us, about an ultimately important reality that cannot be explained by logical and consistent words. For believers who do not understand this, the teaching of Jesus on the Kingdom of God is often reduced to one or another reasonable, but narrow, concept that is never more than a small part of the truth. And, these narrow thoughts lead to radically different, and tragically incomplete, ways of following Jesus. Is the Kingdom just about the afterlife? Just about the end of history? Only about justice-building and peacemaking on earth? Or, only about being close to God? All of these interpretations of the Kingdom of God touch on aspects of Jesus' teaching. None tell the full story. Thousands of books have been written to grapple with the full story. The most important way I can add to this great body of knowledge and opinion is to share with you a couple of my stories of living within the reality of the Kingdom of God.

Story 1: Prayer as a World Beyond Time

There are many versions of this story. In my later years, I have been living this story nearly every day. I arise from sleep anxious, harried or unfocused. I may immediately remember that I am facing a day overloaded with tasks. Still, time has been set aside for prayer and, even if grudgingly, I take that time. As I pray (read my devotional book, say the Jesus prayer, quiet my mind) and draw close to God in my spiritual practice, I generally remember at a deep emotional level that I am safe and loved. Feeling safe, often I am able to give some part of my pain or my struggles over to God, maybe released through tears. I stay present to God for as long as I can keep the distractions at bay. But when the distractions win, and I am pulled away, I simply notice this fact without judgment, and again choose to be with God. Like Jesus's story of the prodigal son, I turn back to the Father. This cycle of drawing close and backing off may repeat itself quite a number of times. But suddenly, almost surprisingly, I find myself listening and hearing the voice of God. Sometimes I discern my marching orders for the day. This has happened time and time again, yet I am always amazed that God has spoken to me. Returning to the time-bound world, I ask questions like these: Did I really hear/feel/know God's presence and word? Over many years I have learned to answer those questions with a faith-filled, "Yes!"

Often, I arise from prayer focused and energized. I was with God in timelessness. Now, without noticing where one experience ended and the other began, I am back in the world where time exerts control on my life. Yet, the world beyond time has changed the world within time—often my day takes a turn towards focused energy and productivity. Often these days I notice that fear has been replaced by love.

I suspect to many this experience sounds fanciful or illogical. Can human beings exit the experience of time passing, enter timelessness and return to the time-bound world, having been changed by the experience? I answer: Yes. Taking into account how physics and mysticism view time, this makes complete sense.

Story 2: 'Sweet Hour of Prayer'

A couple of years ago, I shared in the experience of despair that millions of Americans felt following our presidential election. Many people that I know are still struggling with this dark cloud that, for some, approaches panic.

I remained in that dark cloud of distress for about a month until finally, early in the morning, I took that dread to God in prayer. I began to say a couple of words to God, but immediately I could not say any more because I was overwhelmed by my own sobbing. It took quite a while to get the pain out of my body and into the timeless world of God's heart. Then and there the struggle that had been eating at me was finally surrendered. When I was done, when the weeping stopped, I found myself listening to the words of the great hymn of faith, "Sweet Hour of Prayer," as if God was singing to me:

> Sweet hour of prayer, sweet hour of prayer, that takes me from a world of care.
> And bids me at thy father's throne, make all my wants and wishes known.
> In seasons of distress and grief, my soul has often found relief.
> And oft escaped the tempter's snare, by thy return, sweet hour of prayer.

The Power of Prayer! Mahatma Gandhi's words ring out to me:

> I am neither a man of letters nor of science, but I humbly claim to be a man of prayer. It is prayer that has saved my life. Without prayer I would have lost my reason a long time ago. If I did not lose my peace of soul, in spite of many trials, it is because the peace came to me from prayer. One can live several days without food, but not without prayer. Prayer is the key to each morning and the lock to every evening. Prayer is the sacred alliance between God and man, in order to be delivered from the clutches of the prince of darkness.

For me, a day that began with weeping ended with joy and I was filled with insight and guidance from beyond time. I began to know what to do in the temporal world in this particular crisis of faith. I arose from prayer with a new way of thinking about what had happened in our country, and the world, and ideas about what to do next. My unmanageable fear and hopelessness was gone.

What do these stories prove? Maybe nothing at all to you. To me, these stories illuminate the meaning of Jesus's proclamations concerning the Kingdom of God and all of his warnings about the end of the age. I believe that these stories illustrate the way that the concept of time, according to physics, is consistent with the spiritual truth Jesus announced concerning the Kingdom of God.

The end of the age is in fact upon us—because it is always upon us.

The Kingdom of God is coming in power—and is already within us and among us in power. At any moment we can plug into that power by being with God in the world beyond time and then carry that power into the world of time, knowing that the time is now. We can then, within the very time that is given to us, commit ourselves to being full-fledged disciples of Jesus who, with the community of all others so dedicated, effect salvation in history among all the nations and all of creation. I believe this is what Martin Luther King Jr. meant when he talked about "the Beloved Community." Just as he described it, that Beloved Community is far away—yet we can feel it right now among us. Together, possessed by a transformed consciousness, we can become the key that unlocks the doors to the Kingdom and a transformed future.

The time is always now. This is the spiritual message from all of our great traditions. Borrowing from our Buddhist and Hindu friends, especially Ram Dass, we must always, "Be here now!"

The current crisis in our world leaves absolutely zero wiggle room for anyone wanting to delay their "Yes," to God. We must act not only on account of God, who is Just Love. We must act also, now, on behalf of suffering humanity, of behalf of the children who will inherit the earth from us, and on behalf of the creation that is decaying as result of our wrong actions.

4

A Thousand Caves

Lord, you have been our dwelling-place in all generations.
Before the mountains were brought forth,
or ever you had formed the earth and the world,
from everlasting to everlasting you are God.
Psalm 90:1-2

Let's travel. Let's go exploring.

Let's begin on a mountainside with a thousand caves. Each dark and deep. Each with hidden mysteries. Each with glorious features easily seen from major routes through the darkness—if you carry a light. Each with narrow passageways requiring time and courage to investigate. Each with hidden recesses no one has ever seen, nor is likely to see because you would have to "beam" into them like a space traveler on the starship Enterprise.

I have always been excited about exploring places, people, philosophies, potentials and possibilities. I have spent many days over many years on many treks. Usually, I grieve when it is time to return home and, soon after settling back into the familiar, I always begin looking forward to the next journey. Even so, there are thousands of excursions I will never begin, and on each outing many passages I will not travel. Within each cave, I will have touched ground in only a tiny fraction of its hollows. Yet, when I reflect on these travels, tell others the stories of my adventures, review the photographs—Oh my! I am overwhelmed with gratitude that I have been guided on all my travels. I have seen what most needed to be viewed and learned what most needed to be shared.

I invite you to join the adventure and encourage you to open your mind to the possibility that you will find something within this chapter that will cause you to change your thinking. For example, one of the early readers of my book manuscript was a marriage and family therapist. After reading this chapter he sent me a note thanking me for including the section on "complementarity" that you will soon be reading. Some of his clients, he added, "desperately need to accept that there is more than one way to look at situations."

This chapter is drawn from conversations between spirituality and science happening in many places. Let's begin with the principle of non-locality because I entered this cave long ago.

Nonlocality

Nonlocality is a principle of quantum physics. I am not aware of any scientific findings that have impacted my spirituality more than this one. Just out of seminary, possessed by a materialistic world view, I learned about some strange observations of the subatomic physical world. I have been telling the story for over 40 years.

Scientists have experimented for many years with gigantic machines called particle accelerators or supercolliders. The machine accelerates two particles from an atom and separates them by a distance that approaches infinity. These particles have negative or positive changes. They are in motion. They spin in one direction or the other, in balance.

Changes in one particle cause changes in the other to retain the stability of the atom. The experimenter causes a change in the movement/spin of one particle. Immediately the scientist observes that the spin of the other particle changes simultaneously—without the passage of time. The two particles are connected to each other—you cannot break their bond. This is called "quantum entanglement." Despite a separation that approaches an infinite distance, "communication" between the particles happens at a speed faster than the speed of light, which is 186,000 miles/second. Physics had taught that this was impossible—until it was observed.

The first time I heard this illustration, I knew intuitively that this description of physical reality had spiritual implications. If reality is governed by seemingly impossible laws, and if everything is connected, then what else that has been said to be impossible then becomes possible? Is the power of prayer to connect us to God, to each other, to healing power and miraculous insight consistent with this new information? If the laws once thought to be inviolable in a materialistic universe do not always apply, then could love be the most powerful force holding the universe together and connecting everything?

That is just the beginning. As I explored and pondered scientific findings over the years, I learned many things that slowly changed my understanding of God. Recently, I learned about a related set of findings about nonlocality: the EPR paradox. EPR refers to Albert Einstein, Boris Podolsky and Nathan Rosen—three renowned physicists who argued that there are "elements of reality" that exist outside the theories of Newtonian physics. I believe Einstein and his friends opened a broad doorway to realizing that our universe is not bound by previous understandings of space-time-matter. Spirituality has been pointing us towards similar understanding of reality for centuries.

Over the years, I have come across many descriptions of nonlocality or quantum entanglement. Two best-selling authors have raised the theme. Madeline L'Engle's beloved novel, *A Wrinkle In Time*, rests on these ideas. Father Richard Rohr has searched this cave in his daily devotionals. One of my ministry colleagues in the American Baptist Churches, Kate Jacobs, wrote me a letter after reading an early draft of this book. She offered her own explanation of how this principle has informed her spirituality:

> *God is there in the human relationships that bind us together and bless our lives. I believe that is where the Holy Spirit moves in power, through a phenomenon called quantum entanglement. Science has shown us that physically the fundamental unit of reality is not the isolated particle but the web, the field, the relationship that binds. Furthermore, any two objects that have ever interacted are forever entangled so that, no matter how far apart they move, the behavior of one influences the other faster than the speed of light—instantaneously—and beyond that the behavior of everything entangled with either.*

Our world has a mysterious universal connectedness that goes beyond what we usually consider physical forces. Yes, Einstein was disturbed by what he called "spooky action at a distance" and some physicists who accept it physically deny that it is operative among human beings. Yet this phenomenon of quantum entanglement that is beyond my comprehension scientifically is pure gift experientially, over and over powerfully present in relationships. Most physicists do agree that 13 plus billion years ago, in the Big Bang that started it all, the universe erupted out of the quantum foam as ONE particle, and proceeded to explode, split, and multiply. That means that a fundamental entanglement includes all matter in the universe, since it was all descended from this proto particle.

We are all connected. Everywhere this web of life binds us together with others so that our prayers on their behalf do not just ascend but reach out. They flow not up to a satellite God to beam down an answer but directly through that web to touch our sisters and brothers who are companions on this journey of life. We are together, we are one, no matter how far apart. While the work is not yet finished, the Apostle Paul is certain of the outcome through the Holy Spirit that binds us all together. Together we can transform this world. Together we are on a journey toward the Kingdom of God. Together we are called to connect and create a world that is good for everyone.

In the Nick of Time

Let's explore another cave. How do I know that the reconciliation of spirituality and science is a matter of life and death?

I know because, for years, my own life was on the proverbial chopping block. More than once, I wanted to die. Depression runs in my extended family on both sides. Stories abound in our family history concerning the suffering of aunts, uncles and cousins. Their pain and trauma have, it seems to me, been directly connected to various dysfunctions like alcoholism, slow suicides and all manner of diminished lives. One of my abiding life questions has been, since my teen years, is there a way out of this depressing cycle?

My answer today: "Yes."

Who showed me the way through this repeating and terrifying crisis? My answer: Psychologists, psychiatrists, pharmacologists, spiritual teachers and guides, and above all, God experienced as unconditional love. Together, spirituality and science possessed enough of the truth to foster healing and uplift me towards abundant life.

However, at the beginning—my earliest memory of depression is from eighth grade—none of these resources were available to me. I just toughed it out. My family's religious culture mocked counseling. Our form of religion demonized psychiatry. Family frightened me away from both illegal and legal drugs. My emotional health was dominated by a fear of abandonment. My image of God was one of *conditional* love. Fear was at the heart of my life story.

In college in 1969, counseling became a resource and remained so for many years. In my 30s, spiritual practices of Lectio Divina and prayer—as well as wisdom found in books such as Henri Nouwen's *The Wounded Healer*—supplemented lessons I was learning at conferences, including teaching by Walter Wink and Morton Kelsey.

Eventually, my maturing spirituality led me toward a radically renovated image of God. The distant and angry God began to be, in the hidden depths of my soul, the "available and adoring God." I learned, am still learning, to take all kinds of pain to God in prayer and leave it there, at least until the next time. I have also come to embrace the valuable contribution of science through psychiatry and medications. Now, I counsel others that healing always requires a body-mind-spirit partnership—and I continue to grieve for those who believe that in this area of healing, spirituality and science are enemies.

The Anthropic Principle

The anthropic principle is a widely accepted theory within the science of astrophysics. I believe this theory is consistent—just like the principle of nonlocality—with what I believe, experience and know about God. The principle holds that we can observe only those things in the universe that are conducive to our existence as observers. That makes good sense. Scientists can only perceive those things their senses can measure or test as human researchers.

Huston Smith takes this idea and connects it to the fragile balance that makes our existence possible in the universe. He writes, "If the mathematical ratios in nature had been the slightest bit different, life could not have evolved. Were the force of gravity the tiniest bit stronger, all stars would be blue giants, while if it were slightly weaker, all would be red dwarfs, neither of which would come close" to supporting life. Smith adds that physicists of the stature of John Polkinghorne set the improbability figures for our existence only through the action of chance to be about 1 in 10-followed-by-40-zeroes. British astronomer Sir Fred Hoyle points out in *The Intelligent Universe* that the anthropic principle shatters the common belief that we live in a materialistic universe.

Scientist Dale Kohler wrote, "We have been scraping away at physical reality all these centuries, and now the layer of the remaining little that we don't understand is so thin that God's face is staring right at us."

Chance is not the governing force of our universe. Random events do not determine our fate. Call it what you will, what your beliefs and experiences compel you to name it. I call it Christ, from whom all things come and in whom all things hold together.

Chaos Theory

For a moment, let's explore the cavern of chaos theory, a subset of mathematics that concerns itself with the unpredictability of complex systems, like the weather or organisms or even the stock market. Chaos theory has determined that even the most minute changes at the beginning of a process cause very big changes at the end. A tiny inaccuracy at the beginning, like a number rounded off from four decimal points to two decimal points, causes a huge error at the end.

So what? So, when a scientist or mathematician is trying to predict something, like the weather for a Saturday afternoon baseball game, it is impossible to get the prediction exactly right. Weathermen deserve far less blame than we assign to them. We may know a lot about an organism or any system like a national election, but the most minute fragment of misinformation could ruin the reputation of the prognosticator.

Many people who think they know nothing about chaos theory actually have heard about one of its insights: "the butterfly effect." The idea first showed up in a 1952 Ray Bradbury short story that something as tiny as the death of a butterfly could change history. While there have been a host of other fictional uses of this idea—the core principle has subsequently been adopted by scientists. The future is influenced by so many factors that no one and no machine can know enough to predict it.

I believe that the pure Spirit of Love, in the beginning, before time and space, set everything in motion. Love is the "in the beginning" and the "forever" force that holds all things together. Love is manifest in all processes of growth and change, no matter how complex the systems, and is present in all living systems as design and purpose. But, this presence of Love that affects all systems is not measurable or predictable. It is like the wind, blowing where it will. Love operates outside of anyone's control, so the future will always be unknowable. Love, though uncontrolled, is always acting upon life and we human beings, created by and for Love, change the future each, and every, time Love is manifest in us.

Remember, we know from chaos theory that the impact of unmeasurables—like faith, courage and love—on a complex system does not have to be huge to make a huge difference. And, we can never know exactly what difference that will be. My daughter Lauren has near infinite faith in the potential of Love. As a foster parent she knows that children will come and go into her home and family. Though others will think that her effort to love those children is insignificant, perhaps even wasted when they return to wounded family systems, Lauren knows that not even the teeniest act of Love is ever wasted. Love always finds its completion.

Let's talk about healing. Most informed and open-minded 21st century men and women realize that health is not determined by just mechanistic factors. Norman Cousins introduced many of us to the power of laughter to heal our bodies. The testimony that prayer and love and courage and hope and faith impact health in positive ways has been established with a preponderance of evidence. However, no matter how much of the energy of laughter, prayer, love, courage, hope and faith are brought to bear on a broken body, their impact is uncontrollable and unpredictable. They become part of the chaos of a complex system that determines health results. Sometimes, but not all times, these and other forces for healing—like medications, surgery and the body's recuperative powers—coalesce into healing. Sometimes not. That's the way it is.

Complementarity

A great advance in the ever-expanding science of physics was the determination of the principle of complementarity. The idea is simple, reveals deep truth, yet seems to defy logic. The law of complementarity affirms the theory that two distinct ways of understanding reality can both be true and that each may contribute insight to the other. The idea was developed by Nobel Prize-winning physicist Niels Bohr to describe the inability to measure all properties at the same time in quantum physics. Whatever we can know at any given time—we also know that there's even more we still don't know.

I apply this principle to spirituality and science and conclude that a spiritual belief and scientific theory can both be true, and of value to the other, even if they seem impossibly contradictory. A medical doctor, feeling deep compassion for a woman who is hopelessly near death, turns to prayer. The patient lives. The doctor surrenders to the impossible contradiction between his scientific training and his experience that prayer and compassion may have played a role in the healing. In that moment of despair over the impending death of his patient, the doctor operated for a time as if another view of reality also was true. Of course, we know that many doctors and scientists do pray. Both perspectives often are necessary to adequately understand and respond to reality. There is no longer a need to ignore inconvenient evidence.

Evolution

Evolution is difficult for me, simply because deep change is difficult. I am thinking now of the evolution of my family, the continuing deep change that has been relentlessly advancing in my extended family, whether I like it or not. This evolution has often proceeded as dreamed.

My children are married and have children of their own. Wonderful! And, I have often had to make adjustments, sometimes painful alterations, in my expectations. They no longer "come home" for Christmas. They have homes and lives of their own. Relationships are unpredictable and frequently beyond any control of mine.

Evolution is a universal process. Unfolding is everywhere, within everyone, and all the time. Significant change is around every corner. Evolution is at the heart of the Great Story, the Universal Story, the Cosmic Love Story. There is no universe, and thus no life, without evolution.

Evolution, unfortunately, has often been a battleground. Some Christians regard Darwinism as the enemy. Some scientists regard religion as ignorant. In fact, when I introduce the topic of spirituality and science among Christians, I often encounter the assumption that I am about to fight the newest battle in culture wars that divide us.

Can't we move on? Let me put this bluntly: Evolution is a fact in the same way that Earth revolves around the sun is a fact. Everything evolves. Life evolves. The important questions that need to be at the center of the conversations between spirituality and science are: What do we know about that process, and how do we know it? Is it only science that has a contribution to make in the search for truth or does faith have access to truths of a different sort?

These questions have never been difficult for me. God is the Creator. Evolution is the process. Natural selection and random mutation have only a limited role to play in the evolution of life. Darwin knew that. Truth related to the emergence of life on the planet Earth is only found in the midst of respectful dialog.

The strident debate must end within Christianity, and all other spiritual traditions if humanity is to survive and thrive. Thomas Berry gives us his insight on how critical this issue is when he writes, "We will not be able to move into an ecologically sustainable future on the resources of the existing religious traditions—and we cannot get there without them." Michael Dowd adds his conclusion that nothing is more important to the future of humanity than all of the religions of mankind developing new expressions of faith that include a healthy relationship to Earth and the cosmos. The key to Christianity's reform into such a faith is the remembrance of the Christ who, beginning billions of years ago, brought all things into being and continues to hold all things together.

The Creator is God. One aspect of the process is evolution. The driving force is and always has been and always will be love.

5

Reading Genesis Again—
for the First Time

The heavens are telling the glory of God;
and the firmament proclaims his handiwork.
Day to day pours forth speech,
and night to night declares knowledge.
There is no speech, nor are there words;
their voice is not heard;
yet their voice goes out through all the earth,
and their words to the end of the world.

Psalm 19:1-4, NRSV

Way back in my seminary days, I was doing field education at the Baptist church in Williamson, NY. Together with the village's Presbyterians, we were at the beginning of a Lay Witness Mission weekend. Informal conversation turned toward Genesis. All I did was contribute my contrary opinion. Explosion!

Back further in time, my brother John and I were about to enroll in Owego Free Academy in Owego, NY. The superintendent of schools called my mom and dad. Dad had just succeeded a fundamentalist pastor at the First Baptist Church. The superintendent, soon to become Dad's friend, was hoping to dodge controversy by offering options to my parents. John and I could be excused from physical education class when they were teaching square dancing and from biology class when they were introducing evolutionary theory. Mom and Dad respectfully declined. The strictures, legalisms and prohibitions common to many Baptists had no roots in our family. We danced, played cards and went to movies.

When I became a Baptist pastor myself, I began dodging Genesis. That worked pretty well for 40 years and a couple of thousand sermons.

Early in 2018, deep into my research on spirituality and science, I could no longer avoid Genesis. These earliest accounts needed to become part of a solution to a much bigger problem: How do we get past the evolutionist-creationist controversy? The stories of Genesis 1-11 have shaped our worldview and our operational images of God. They have convinced many that we live on a very young Earth (only thousands of years old) and that human beings are the dominators of creation—the solitary pinnacle of the purposes of God. This world view has supported human activity that uses and abuses the rest of the Earth community. The extinction of thousands of plant and animal species is viewed as a necessary and morally justified consequence of this activity. Take from the Earth; destroy the land, air, water and beauty. Take no thought about tomorrow's children.

Worse yet, the stories of Genesis 1-11 have been abused to perpetuate images of God and beliefs about humanity that have wounded bodies, minds and spirits of generations of precious children of God. They also violate what we learn about magnificence of creation, the unmeasurable love of God, and humanity's place in the unfolding purposes of God within the creation. In the evangelical world, we teach our children to sing, "Jesus loves the little children … they are precious in His sight." Then, many Christians go on to teach these same children that they are born in sin, depraved. In this religious mindset, we proclaim to our children the unconditional love of God—then teach them that the vast majority of human beings who once lived on Earth are now suffering unimaginable eternal torment because they thought the wrong thoughts or were born in the wrong place. We read them the repeating verses that God sees the creation and creatures to be very good. Then we destroy that goodness and claim that this destruction is of no consequence. We teach children about the love made manifest in Jesus of Nazareth 2,000 years ago but avoid mention that in and through Christ this love has been doing its work in all things everywhere for over 13 billion years.

Consider the opening verses of Psalm 19 that you read at the beginning of this chapter. God is everywhere to be found. Even where no words are spoken concerning Jesus, Christ shines forth from the heavens. God not only spoke the creation into being. God continues speaking. Yet far too many Christians remain deaf and blind to these truths.

The first nations who inhabited the American continents were—and still are—among the most sensitive hearers of the word proclaimed by the heavens. They knew how to live as one with every sacred thing that God made. Since college, when I wrote an independent study paper that included insights from First Nations spirituality, their eyes and ears have sharpened the acuity of mine. With the guidance of all perceivers of Truth—seekers from other spiritual traditions—I have learned that I can look and listen and know Truth as it is revealed everywhere.

Reading Genesis 1-11 for the First Time

Even if you grew up learning these chapters of Genesis almost by heart—it still is possible to read the stories in chapters 1-11 again, as if for the first time. The same goes for other portions of the Scriptures. You can, if you so choose, listen for a word of the Lord as fresh as the new day, hear God's speaking to you and respond to a clear and intimate word of God.

Mostly, however, we prefer to settle for the old and stale word, spoken to someone else, at another time, in a life situation far removed from our own. Mostly we don't even believe that God can speak an appetizing word directly to us that feeds body, mind and spirit. In fact, it is possible to rediscover a word that is so nurturing that is breathes life into us, fills us and opens us up to new possibilities. This is a challenge in all the world's religious traditions these days. Fresh readings are especially critical in the opening chapters of Genesis because no text has become more divisive among the world's 2 billion Christians, threatening our fellowship and diminishing our witness to the world.

For the nation of Israel, the creation story and all the stories from the first 11 chapters of Genesis, are stories about God and God's children. Especially important to Israel was the command, "Thou shalt have no other gods before me" (Exodus 20:3, NRSV). Revealing God to the nations, believing and telling the truth of God, became the mission of the People of God. It still is. So, Israel told the stories of God and proclaimed the message that God is Creator. The creation is good. God is Love. Nothing is to rule our lives except God. All of creation emerged from a single source. We are connected. All of God's children are one. All of us are the human race.

The work of reinterpreting Genesis is both timely and urgent, so let's get started.

To begin, simply choose the Scripture you desire to read afresh. A few verses at a time is best. Turning to that text, I ask God to speak to me as I am reading so that God's word can become as personal and real to me as the air I breathe. I may pray, "Lord of Life, as I read today speak to my mind and my heart and my soul your living word for my life and for my writing." At that point, I have already been thinking about the text, what has been taught to me in the past and what the experts and the commentaries have told me. But I seek to set these thoughts aside for a while. I ask God to speak to me, right now, to reveal God's word, as if for the first time. I begin by simply reading the text. Then I read it again, this time aloud. Then I read it again, as if I am soaking in the sun on a beautiful summer's day. I may pray again, asking God for eyes that see and a mind open to wisdom.

Almost always I will read the text in different translations, taking notes on the differences in wording that I may choose to pay attention to later. I may take a minute to reflect on what I have just read. I may write down words, images or thoughts on which God invites me to focus. I ask questions, like, "How is this word of God, that caught my attention, important in my life, to my readers and to the world?"

I continue to take notes, recording the experiences and situations that this word of the Lord brings to mind and the questions it lifts up. Sometimes I enter a time of waiting on the Lord that may last seconds or minutes or even days. When it's time to pray again, I ask for God's continuing guidance as I reflect upon the text and consider the connections between the word and our lives. Eventually it will be the right time to remember anything that I have learned about this text in the past, to consider what others taught me and to consult a Bible commentary or two. At this point I also like to consult with the community of faith, allowing others to challenge me and support me. Don't let any of the books or experts tell you what you must think or believe. At the same time, do be open to their correction, allow them to suggest possibilities and add to your understanding.

That's essentially how I approach reading a text again for the first time. New life circumstances. New openness. New insights. A new and personal word of the Lord for you on a new day.

This way of reading the Bible actually is many centuries old and is often called *lectio divina* or holy reading. *Lectio divina* is not an easy process. I do not pursue this practice perfectly. Sometimes I have to start all over again to listen to God. Often that occurs because the people and books I consult convince me that my reading and listening had not been adequate.

For further guidance in reading Genesis again for the first time, check out the fourth century desert fathers and mothers, the rule of St. Benedict, and the writings of St. John of the Cross. For guidance in your reading and application of the Genesis stories, consider Danielle Shroyer's book, *Original Blessing*, and Walter Brueggemann's commentary, *Genesis: Interpretation: A Bible Commentary for Teaching and Preaching.* The works of 20th century Jewish scholar Rabbi Abraham Joshua Heschel can also provide valuable guidance in understanding how the Jewish fathers and mothers of our faith read and interpreted Scripture and encountered God in the sacred texts. I also must acknowledge the debts I owe the Rev. Cynthia Bourgeault and Father Richard Rohr. They have been ever present within my thinking, writing and spiritual journey. At the "Trinity conference" in the spring of 2016, their teaching deepened my understanding of "The Christ."

We all have a point of view from which we read Scripture. In my encounters with Scripture I long to see through the eyes of Jesus. Father Rohr has done a great deal of writing that encourages us to learn to read and interpret the Bible the way Jesus encountered and applied sacred texts. He reminds us that Jesus participated in the Jewish practice of *midrash*, a discipline that asks questions, promotes dialogue and opens the reader to new spiritual awareness and faithful understanding. Jesus even ignored texts that promoted exclusion and violence and focused on Scripture that promoted unity, inclusion, mercy and integrity.

In the following chapters, I will take a similar approach as we engage the stories in the first 11 chapters of Genesis. As always, my objective is to see if we can encounter the God who is Just Love. When we personally know this God, we will be able to pass on faith, hope and love to the next generation.

During the *lectio divina* process on Genesis, I also was learning from scientists. I met with biologist J. Scott Turner, after reading his carefully crafted book: *Purpose and Desire: What Makes Something "Alive" And Why Modern Darwinism Has Failed to Explain It*. Both his scholarship and his faith deepened my commitment to doing all I can to contribute to a new and life-giving partnership between spirituality and science. I also kept returning to *Code Name God: The Spiritual Odyssey of a Man of Science*, by physicist Mani Bhaumik, whose work was instrumental in building the science behind LASIK surgery. His journey in science first took him away from his Hindu roots, and eventually led him back to an awareness of the indispensable unity between spirituality and science.

God's Love in Our Perilous Times

Why is this process of rediscovering God's love so crucial right now? Because faith is an indispensable resource when we come face to face with danger, tragedy, the unknown and a host of other perils we could not have imagined yesterday.

In our daily lives, we are assaulted by a nearly infinite variety of fears. Here are just a few of the hundreds referred to me by social media friends:

My boss.

Moving.

The police.

Losing a game.

The death of my spouse.

A power outage.

Failure.

Success.

Floods.

Bee stings.

Climate change.

Losing my sight.

Someone yelling at me.

Rejection.

Displeasing my mother.

The future for my children.

Being falsely accused.

Being useless.

Eating in public.

Teachers.

My kids driving.

Tornadoes.

God's judgment.

That's just a sampling of the far longer list I compiled from friends! How do we live in such a perilous a world?

Our faith teaches us: Perfect love casts out fear. It's right there in 1 John 1:18.

God's love is perfect. My own faith in God's perfect love is not perfect— but it has been heading in that direction for a very long time. These days I experience far less fear than I did in the past. Now, I have many ways to get beyond fear when it does attack. I climb one version or another of my seeing tree. I simply remember that I am infinitely and unconditionally loved by God. Sometimes I talk out the fear with a friend. Other times I voluntarily dive deep into the fear, but only within the presence of God, encased in love.

Christians often describe this being with God's presence as being "in Christ." I am convinced that we can only be fully "in Christ" when we know the full story of Christ. For me that involves knowing Christ in three distinct and equally important ways:

1. Christ with God before the beginning; Christ the spoken Word of God that brought everything in the universe into being and holds everything together.

2. The incarnate Jesus of Nazareth, known especially in the four Gospels.
3. The Christ of faith with whom deep and abiding friendship is possible.

Scripture tells us of Christ incarnate in Jesus. However, it is science that tells us what the Christ was up to during the billions of years following the beginning of the universe. To tell the full, universal story, religion and science must collaborate in knowing and telling the truth. Working together, we can confront the forces leading our world toward catastrophe. The prophets' voices are all around us.

The times—they are a-changin'.

Bob Dylan

The sky is falling!

Chicken Little

In those days, there will be weeping and gnashing of teeth.

Jesus

Therefore it shall be night to you, without vision.

Micah

So the garden became, by the morning, like a dark and desolate spot.

The Quran

When will we be driven deep into the valley of the shadow of death? No one knows for certain. But soon. How deep will the darkness be? No one knows for certain. But too deep to extricate ourselves. What will break us? War? Famine? Rising sea levels? Economic collapse? No one knows for certain. What is certain is that fear will grab hold of us and attempt to suck us into its abyss.

Our hope lies in living very close to God who is Just Love.

6

Love, in the Beginning

No one has ever seen God.
If we love one another, God lives in us,
And his love is perfected in us.
1 John 4:12

Where do we start to learn and share the truth that God Is Just Love? Finally, an easy question!

Let's start at the very beginning.
A very good place to start.

Somehow God, the Pure Spirit of Love, brought the world of space, time, matter and energy into existence. Pure and Infinite and Eternal Spirit was altered, converted, transformed, transmuted into a creation, a finite world of time and space and matter and energy, and us! How did God do that? None of us—not even those with magnificent minds and deep spirits—will ever answer that question. The Bible simply tells us that God "said" something. God "spoke" the entire universe into being. In Genesis 1:3, God says: "Let there be light."

So, let's spend some time thinking about how we can talk to our children about light. One of my favorite stories concerns all the animals in the forest. In the beginning of this story, all the animals experienced was darkness. Ask your children what it would be like to live all the time in darkness. How would they feel? Ask them how many of them prefer to sleep with a night light on or the door cracked open.

Near the beginning of time, the animals in the great forest called a council of all the critters, great and small. Every animal was to have a voice at this council because the decision to be made would change all of their lives. The purpose of the council was to decide if there would be light in the midst of their dark forest.

Bear, thinking of himself as the most powerful animal in the world, spoke first. Bear growled, "We must have darkness!"

Most of the other animals seemed to lose their voices because they were frightened by bear. But there was a young and foolish chipmunk at the council. We will call him Chip. Sure, Chip was afraid of the gruff and powerful bear, but not so afraid that he could not speak. He climbed up on top of a rock so he could be seen and simply chirped, "Let there be light."

Bear growled.

Chip sang this time, "Let there be light!" The other animals could not believe their ears. They all stared at Chip as he kept singing, "Let there be light!"

Bear growled again, and this time he reached out a great paw with very sharp claws. Chip dodged just in time, but not fast enough to prevent Bear from scraping a stripe on the chipmunk's back. To this day chipmunks have a stripe on their backs to remind all the animals to have courage.

As he dodged the bear's pursuit, he kept singing, "Let there be light, let there be light, let there be light in this dark world."

Suddenly, all the animals began to sing, "Let there be light, let there be light, let there be light in this dark world."

Do you know what happened next? That's right. All the animals looked toward the east. They saw the sun rising in the sky. Ever since then, the world has experienced both day and night. The light has many names. Some call it courage. I call this light,

"Love." When I am afraid, I can sing, "Let there be light, let there be light, let there be light in this dark world!"

Now, after you have shared that story with your children, you might want to return to the story in the Bible where we learn of the very moment when God made light and separated the light from the darkness and called the time of light "day" and called the time of darkness, "night." To help children grasp with wonderment the miracle of light, you would be hard-pressed to find a better resource than two children's books by Matthew Paul Turner, *When God Made the World* and *When God Made Light*. I love these books. More important, my grandchildren love them!

Personalize the story for your children. "When God made you—Alison, Noah, John and Sara—God made light!" Reinforce the story with songs like:

Cover my light with a basket, No!
I'm going to let it shine!
Cover my light with a basket, No!
I'm going to let it shine, let it shine, let it shine, let it shine!

Think about questions we can raise. When God spoke the world into being with the word, "light" How much light was created? When God spoke, was the result something like the beam of light sent forth from a single candle—or from a searchlight? Or was it more like an explosion of intergalactic intensity, brighter than a thousand times a thousand suns? I wasn't there; but I would vote for the explosive light of a million times a billion suns, and that's just for starters.

For Christians, Jesus is often referred to as, "The Light of the World." How does this work, given that Jesus of Nazareth was not born on this earth until more than 13 billion years after God called for light? One place Christians look for answers is the opening passage of the Gospel of John: "In the beginning was the Word, and the Word was with God, and the Word was God. He was in the beginning with God." For Christians, John 1:1-2 testifies to the existence of the Christ, one with the Father even before time. We human beings will never see past the beginning. But, if we could, I believe we would see the Father, the Christ and the Spirit existing as One as an eternal and indissoluble indwelling and out-flowing of Love.

Also, according to John's Gospel, Christ is always available to us: "All things came into being through him, and without him not one thing came into being. What has come into being in him was life, and the life was the light of all people. The light shines in the darkness, and the darkness did not overcome it." (John 1:3-5)

Of course, this is a more expansive understanding of Jesus Christ than was taught for years in most seminaries. It was not until 1988 that Matthew Fox's seminal work, *The Coming of the Cosmic Christ*, so impacted my worldview and my operational theology that I could start grasping the truth that was in the Bible all along. It is interesting to note that even before page 1, Fox quotes mystic Meister Eckhart as saying, "Though we are God's sons and daughters, we did not realize it yet." The 1980s were the season in my life when I first began to realize that, as a child of God, I was unconditionally and unalterably beloved of the Father, Son and Holy Spirit. But it was not until the decade that just ended that, with the inspiration and teaching of Father Richard Rohr, I began to know how to talk of the Christ who is present in all times and places. On first hearing, I fell in love with Rohr's phrase, "A Christian is one who has learned to see Christ everywhere." Father Rohr also introduced me to the theologians and spiritual masters who carried this truth through history, including St. Francis of Assisi who lived this understanding of the Christ, John Duns Scotus (1266–1308) who put this perception into philosophical form, and Teilhard de Chardin, who brought this insight into the modern world.

However, I am not writing only to a circle of philosophers and theologians. I am seeking to reach everyone who loves children with the message, "God is Just Love." So, how do I translate these insights on behalf of the children who need our help to find hope and be love in a future of global perils? The core message of this chapter is that the stories in Genesis 1-11 must be revisited and then translated to help our children experience a new vision of God. That means we need to encourage intergenerational experiences.

Family Cluster, Day 1

I invite you to imagine that you are a member of an intergenerational spiritual education group called a Family Cluster. For many years, I was a leader and trainer in the Family Cluster movement and a follower of its founder, Margaret M. Sawin. Within the context of such groups, we can find ways to revisit, translate and apply Genesis that will work for our children.

Envision a Family Cluster session as opening with a half-mile hike through the woods, everyone carrying sack lunches and drinks and, after a while, some of the younger children. Bobbie, age 6, is on my shoulders. We are about to leave the woods and enter a stunning meadow full of sunlight and wildflowers. In the center of the meadow is a campfire circle. I remind our group of 12 adults, nine children and three teens that we are to enter the meadow quietly. The six volunteers for today's center circle are to sit around the campfire. Everyone else forms an outer circle.

After two minutes of silence in this lush meadow, my co-leader Shari asks those in the center circle, "What kinds of feelings come up for you while sitting here quietly?"

Mostly they share how much each one enjoyed the silence, the joy of listening to the chirping birds, the comfort of hearing the soft sound of wind through the trees. Lots of gratitude to God is expressed. One mother thanks her child for sharing the silence and allowing her these moments of peace.

Shari then asks the center group, sometimes called the "Magic Circle," to reflect on silence in their everyday lives. The conclusion of the group is that silence is both needed and pretty much nonexistent. But, one of the children does share how much he sometimes enjoys the discipline of "time out." Sharing ends and we all gather in the larger circle.

I ask Grandpa Paul to read today's Scripture. He holds up a poster with the words of Genesis 1:1 printed neatly and reads the text. "In the beginning God created the heavens and the earth."

I add that tomorrow we will be talking about what God created and what God loves. But today I ask the group, "What was God doing before the beginning?"

Everybody looks around. No one speaks, until Josh, one of the teens, cracks: "If I had been God, I would have been enjoying all the quiet—the silence before the big bang of creation and the noise and complaints of all the people."

Laughter ensues, of course.

Shari responds, "Yes, Josh, God may have been enjoying the silence just like we did today."

I say, "Let's form a big circle, holding hands. Now, everyone, walk to the left. Keep walking. Now go faster. Faster still. Keep going. Don't let go! Faster. Faster!"

The children giggle. The teens shout, "Faster!" The adults shout, "Slow down!" Suddenly, one of the grandparents lets go. The circle flies apart. Some sit on the grass. Others crash and roll. What joy. What exuberance.

We all sit back down in the circle, catching our breath. I say: "Could it be that before the beginning, God was laughing joyfully? Could it be that God the Father was just loving?"

Another of the teens, Felice, questioned me: "Who was God loving? You can't love if there is no one to love."

I direct this question to the group, asking them who God might have been loving.

I hear whispers. "Jesus." "The Holy Spirit."

I suggest, "What if God the Father, the Son Jesus and the Holy Spirit were like us, holding hands, running in a circle, faster and faster, generating more and more love, until there was so much extra love that it could not be contained in Heaven and had to explode forth and make a world?"

Shari announces that we've asked Felice to read everyone a story about what it might have looked like and felt like when God's love burst forth from Heaven to make a world. Felice stands with the book in hand and begins to share the words and the pictures. Highly recommended here is the children's book, *Before The Beginning: A Child's First Book of the Great Story*, by JD Stillwater. There are other choices and the ages of your children might help you decide what to read to them.

Family Cluster, Day 2

Now, let's return to this example of a Family Cluster camp for our next lessons on how the Genesis stories can be revisited, translated and applied to the lives of our children.

It's raining cats and dogs outside, but before the children can begin complaining about a boring day, I organize a quick group game with enough movement and laughter to burn off some of the energy. Then we slide quickly into a series of wild animal songs—that is, wild songs about all kinds of animals. Josh breaks the group into wild laughter when he suggests that Old McDonald had a gorilla on his farm!

One of the younger boys turns to his father and asks, "Can we visit the gorilla farm?" More laughter.

Suddenly, 5-year-old Mattie is furiously waving her hands. "Let's sing about sharks!"

"I'm sorry, I don't play any shark songs."

"You don't need to play," she answers with a smirk on her face. "I will lead it." Mattie jumps up, stands in the middle of the circle, and shouts, "Anybody want to help?" All the children jump up—even a couple of the mothers. Suddenly we are deep into the words and the motions of:

> *Baby shark, da do, da do, da da …*
> *Mama shark …*
> *Daddy shark …*

At the end of "Baby Shark," Shari quickly announces that Mattie's father will be sharing our Bible reading today. Benjamin picks up a poster, places it on the easel and reads Genesis 2: 19-20c: "So out of the ground the LORD God formed every animal of the field and every bird of the air and brought them to the man to see what he would call them; and whatever the man called every living creature, that was its name. The man gave names to all cattle, and to the birds of the air, and to every animal of the field …"

Benjamin then explains that Adam named the animals because God wanted Adam and the animals to be friends. Forever and ever, it would be humanity's job to take care of the animals, and the plants, and every-thing on the Earth. That was our first job. It is still the most important job God has given us—to take care of the Earth and to take care of each other.

I continue, "Thanks Benjamin. It's time to form our Magic Circle, and you already know that our topic today is our friendships with animals. Billy and his mom will be the leaders in our circle today. Billy is going to be talking about the animals on his farm and Billy's mom, who teaches biology, is going to be sharing a few things she has learned about what is happening to animals in our world. And, please remember, there is an open seat in the center circle. At any time, any of us in the outer circle can go into the inner circle, wait our turn, speak and then return to the outer circle.

Billy begins. "We have a strict rule on our farm. Some of our animals are pets and we give them names, like our dog, Scout, and the cats, Salt and Pepper. We also give names to cows we milk and they each have very different personalities. They become our friends. I especially like Milkmaid because she always tries to lick me when I walk by. They take care of us and we take care of them. We also raise animals that will become food for us and others, food like chicken and bacon from pigs. We try to remember to be grateful for them and we do our best to make sure that the chickens live like they were meant to live, not cramped up in a coop. But we don't name them because someday we will have to kill them for food. That's the way it is on a farm."

Blair, Billy's mother, continues. "Billy did not mention some of the other animals that visit our farm. They are wild animals, like the fox. Foxes eat other animals, like mice and chipmunks. That's just the way it is for some animals. But if the foxes are hungry enough, they will sneak onto our farm in the darkness of the night and try to catch one of our chickens. That's why the chickens are fenced in at night."

She brings out a poster and explains, "Animals that eat other animals are called C-A-R-N-I-V-O-R-E-S. Animals that eat only plants and berries and things like that are called, H-E-R-B-I-V-O-R-E-S. Some animals eat both other animals and plants. They are called O-M-N-I-V-O-R-E-S. Can you think of animals that eat both?"

Molly says, "Bears."

"Yes, Molly, that's right," Blair says. "Bears eat both other animals and plants. That's what they are supposed to do. That's how God made them. Any other answers?"

Someone calls out, "People."

"Yes, that's also right. People—at least some people—eat both animals and plants. There are many people, however, who choose not to eat other animals. Do you know what they are called?"

"Healthy," says Thomas.

"OK, that is a good answer. But a more general answer is, V-E-G-E-T-A-R-I-A-N-S. Vegetarians don't eat other animals because they believe that is a healthier way and a good way to live. Are there any vegetarians in our group?"

One family of five raises their hands.

A teen from another family says, "I only eat chicken and seafood."

Blair continues, "On our farm, animals like chickens, pigs and cattle are killed so that people can have food. However, millions of other animals die in the world because people are careless and greedy. People take the land where the animals used to live; that's called habitat destruction. Other people hunt and kill so many animals on the land or catch so many animals in the ocean that those groups of animals—they are called species—disappear forever. Pollution of the air and the water kills millions of animals, plants too. They disappear forever. So, now, let's talk about the animals we love and how it makes us feel that so many are dying."

This discussion in the inner circle goes on longer than we had expected. One person after another in the outer circle enters that inner circle, speaks and returns to the outer circle until everyone in our Family Cluster has had a say. Some more than once. There are many tears and expressions of anger, regret and even hopelessness.

Shari and I look at each other and decide to cancel the rest of the activities for this session. Shari says, "Let's all stand, make a circle, hold hands and pray. I will start. Anyone can add a prayer. Ken, will you close our prayer time when it's time?" The prayers are very emotional. The grief and anger expressed by some in our group was thick enough to be cut with a knife.

Shari and I stay up late that night, redesigning the next day's session. We decided to dispense with all the opening activities for the next day, except breakfast, and asked everyone to meet us right after breakfast in our meeting room. We set up tables in that room in the form of a rectangle with spaces between the tables, making it easy to enter the inner space. We cover the floor with every old magazine we can find, especially dozens of back issues of *National Geographic*. We cover the tables with sheets of newsprint, and then an array of markers, crayons, paints, glue, glitter, construction paper, string, coat hangers, sticks and tapes of all kinds.

Finally, it is time to crash. However, shortly after turning out the lights, a knock on my cabin door is thunderous. *Boom, boom!* Again. *Boom!* Shari, shouts, "Ken, get up, you have to see this!"

I throw on my jeans, unlock the door and protest that it is one o'clock in the morning. Shari exclaims, "You have to see this! Everyone has to see this!" She explains that she had been unable to sleep because of all the intense emotions expressed in our session, so she had wandered down to the lake. There she encountered a glorious display of the northern lights roaming around the sky.

Wondrous.

Shari asks me: "Do we wake everyone up?"

"Well, yes, at least the adults," I answer with more certainty than was reasonable for such a time, "The adults can decide for themselves about their children."

No more than 20 minutes later our entire Family Cluster group, every single member including a couple of still-asleep toddlers, is lying side by side on the beach, holding hands, beholding the marvels of creation: a star-filled nighttime sky, the very visible Milky Way galaxy, and in the northern sky a display of color that takes everyone's breath away.

The wondrous sky is a healing balm washing over all of us.

Shari tells me, on the walk back to the cabins, that the next morning she is going to change the directions for our morning activity. I tell her, "Go for it—but I'm going back to bed."

Is it possible for wonderment, joy, gratitude, community and love to exist, side by side, at one and the same time, with regret, despair, grief, loneliness, emptiness? Is it possible for hope and love to dwell side by side with suffering?

Shari begins our gathering the next morning by reminding us that the first job God gave us was to take care of the creation, to be friends with the animals and the plants and the entire Earth. With everyone in obvious agreement, she adds, "We have not been doing such a good job with that. You and I can do better." Then Shari suggests that there is another job God has given us. Human beings have eyes, ears, minds, hearts and souls. We can see beauty. We can recognize the grandeur of God's creation. We can celebrate life and give thanks. We can feel wonderment.

"Last night, we had an unforgettable experience of that wonderment," she says. "We saw the great gift of the northern lights, even if we had to get up in the middle of the night to do so. We felt deep sadness and deep thankfulness, all in one day. Maybe life can be painful and delightful all at the same time."

Then, Shari gives her instructions for the morning in our room filled with arts and crafts supplies. "Create something—a poster, a drawing, a collage, a mobile—that shows what you have been experiencing here during the last 24 hours. Your friendships. Your sadness for the animals. The awe that has touched you. The hope that is in your hearts. Tell us about the animals and the people you love. Tell us what you fear. Be real."

Not another word of guidance is needed. It takes the rest of the morning to create our presentations.

We share many marvelous stories that day, both visually and verbally. Here's just one of them: Lauren, the girl who earlier said she only eats plants plus poultry and fish, is 11 years old. She told us her story. She had scoured all the magazines for pictures of every animal she could find and had created a zoological masterpiece. When she couldn't find an aardvark, she drew a picture of one. Some of the species of animals had many varieties. There were so many of them that they were hung on long strings from the bottom of her collage. The strange thing, though, was that she had added an overlay of crosses. There were all kinds of crosses. String and stick crosses. Painted and glitter crosses. Crosses drawn with crayons and with colored pencils. Crosses cut out of construction paper and cloth. One for each of her animals.

After we all spend quiet moments simply taking in her complex artwork, Lauren explains why she added those crosses: "Inside every animal is a cross. Christ created everything and is inside everything. Jesus lives in every animal. Every animal is love."

More silence follows her explanation. Emotion is obvious in hugs among family members and friends.

Then, Shari asks about other geometric symbols on this collage. "What about these triangles?"

"Those mark all the animals who have died away because we destroyed their world," Lauren says.

"And the blue circles?" Shari asks.

Lauren pauses. "Those are my tears. I wonder if I can ever have all the tears they deserve."

That's when Bobbie steps up and tells her, "You can use some of mine."

7

How Good Is Good Enough?

God said, "Let us make humankind in our image, according to our likeness; and let them have dominion over the fish of the sea, and over the birds of the air, and over the cattle, and over all the wild animals of the earth, and over every creeping thing that creeps upon the earth."

So God created humankind in his image, in the image of God he created them, male and female he created them. ...

God saw everything that he had made, and indeed, it was very good. And there was evening and there was morning, the sixth day.

Genesis 1:26-27 and 31

God says that male and female humans are, along with the rest of creation, "very good"—but is that good enough for God to love all of us always? Many theologians and preachers have been teaching us for many years that we are not good enough for God to love always.

Many churches open worship with a cheer: "God is good! All the time! All the time! God is good!" But is God good enough for all of us to trust God no matter what happens? Is God good enough for us to love God all the time?

We hear complaints such as, "If God loved me, I would not have suffered so." Or, "If I was God, I could have made a better world than this one."

Far too many of us doubt that we are good enough for God to love us all the time. Or, many of us think we have to work very hard just to earn "sometimes love." And, far too many people seem certain that other groups of people—outsiders, foreigners, immigrants, pagans, scape-goats—are never good enough for God to love.

It's easy to trust and love God when things are going our way, but life contains so many ordinary encounters with accidents, tragedies, diseases and death that we quickly can doubt the goodness of God. The problem is that our children need us to teach them, in this era of emerging perils, to reassure them about the love of God. Believing that God is Just Love is the path on which we will recover our sanity and learn to know that we are always good enough for God to love—and God is certainly always good enough to merit our unqualified trust, devotion and worship.

After moving to Ohio, we needed to choose a new church family—make that families. My son Micah's family has been very active at Sanctuary Columbus Church for quite a few years. My daughter Lauren's family has been very active at Heritage Church Columbus for many years. Both churches are an hour from our home. We have been frequent visitors at both. Thank God, both churches are passionate about doing justice, being love and walking very close to God.

Even so, some adjustments are difficult for me. Traditional Christian hymns always have touched my soul, however, both Heritage and Sanctuary excel in their contemporary music. At Heritage on one Saturday evening, we sang *Build My Life* by Housefires, including these lines:

And I will build my life upon your love, it is a firm foundation.
And I will put my trust in you alone and I will not be shaken.

We also sang, *King of My Heart* by Leon Timbo.

You are good, good, oh.
You are good, good, oh.
You're never gonna let me down.
You're never gonna let me down.

I was spiritually, emotionally and physically caught up by the music and the lyrics. I found myself praying that the message of the song would take possession of each and every soul so that, in fact, no matter what the circumstances encountered in life, we believers would know the love of God as a sure foundation.

In our shared Abrahamic tradition, Jews, Christians and Muslims are grounded in the Genesis stories—so, the path toward new thinking about ourselves, goodness and God passes through the Garden of Eden, Adam and Eve, as well as Cain and Abel. Given the anger, treachery and violence in these stories, how can we find anything close to the conclusion that God is Just Love?

Let's return to our Family Cluster camp, taking a fresh look at the Genesis stories.

Family Cluster, Day 3

I start our session with a challenge. "We will be opening our gathering today with a beautiful song. The bad news is that you have to guess the song before we will sing it. The good news is that I will give you three clues. Raise your hand as soon as you think you know the song, but don't guess out loud. OK?"

I say, "Clue 1: This is a beautiful song about love." One hand shoots up. "Barry, you think you know the song just from one clue? Well, don't say it out loud."

Then, I add, "Clue 2: This beautiful song about love is also a song about the Bible." I see lots of hands now. "Hush, don't say a word," I say.

But, I hear a child whisper, "The B-I-B-L-E."

I add, "Clue 3: This beautiful song about love and the Bible is also a song about you." A few more hands, but not everyone is sure yet. "OK, I will give you another clue. Clue 4: This is also a beautiful song about Jesus." I see an explosion of hands. "I am going to count to three and then everyone, yell out the title of the song. 1, 2, 3!"

"Jesus Loves Me!"

We all sing the familiar words:

> *Jesus love me, this I know.*
> *For the Bible tells me so.*
> *Little ones to him belong.*
> *They are weak but he is strong.*
> *Yes, Jesus loves me.*
> *Yes, Jesus loves me.*
> *Yes, Jesus loves me.*

The Bible tells me so.

Many years ago, I wrote a second verse to "Jesus Loves Me":

Jesus loves me, when I'm good—
When I do the things I should.
Jesus loves me when I'm bad—
Though it makes him very sad.

Shari asks, "What do the first and second verses of "Jesus Loves Me" teach us about God and about ourselves and about love? Can I get six volunteers for our circle today to discuss that question?" Then she repeats the instructions about our two concentric circles. "Let's go around the inner circle and give everyone a chance to share. Remember, you can pass. Also remember that it is OK if your answer is the same as someone else's. And, everyone not in the inner circle, remember there is an empty seat that you can occupy long enough to share your answer."

Some of the answers we hear:

"The Bible tells us that Jesus loves us. Jesus knows that we are weak and will make mistakes. Jesus understands that it is hard for us to always do the right thing. Jesus keeps on loving us even when we do wrong."

And: "The second verse says that when we are bad, Jesus is sad, not mad. I would have thought that Jesus would be mad, like my parents get mad at me."

"That's right. As an adult, I do sometimes get mad. That is often because I am weak, too. I get scared or frustrated. Sometimes I am just tired and mad. But, Jesus never stops loving us."

I ask, "Is there anyone in the whole world who is not included in the chorus, 'Yes, Jesus loves me'?"

That's my cue to tell a story:

"We are meeting in the flower garden today. And, the story I am about to tell you begins in a garden. The first two children named in the Bible who are loved by God are Adam and Eve. What do you know about Adam and Eve? Yes, they made a big mistake. Do you think God was mad at them? Or, maybe God was just sad?

"I think God was sad. There are consequences to many of our mistakes. Adam and Eve have to leave the garden where life is easy and go into a world where life is much harder. But before they leave, does anyone remember what God gives to his children, Adam and Eve? God gives them durable and warm clothes to replace their fig leaves. Why do you think God did that? Yes, God loved them. God wanted them to be safe. What would you think about parents who told you that that they were going to take you snow sledding on the hill behind your house, and then handed you a pair of shorts, a T-shirt and sandals to wear? Yeah, you might think they didn't care. Or, that they were very careless or maybe just plain stupid. Well, God was not stupid, careless or unloving. God gave Adam and Eve the right clothes. The children of God would never go to any place where God would not care for them.

"But now we come to a much more difficult part of the Genesis story. Adam and Eve had two children who grew up to be strong young men. Their names were Cain and Abel. Like Billy's family, they both were farmers. For thousands of years, that is what most of the people on the earth did for a living. They planted and harvested crops and they raised animals for food and to help with the work—like oxen pulling a plough.

"Have you ever heard the phrase, "attitude of gratitude?" There is a song often sung in churches about the attitude of gratitude. Paula is going to play her guitar and sign this song for us."

> *We plow the fields and scatter*
> *The good seed on the land,*
> *But it is fed and watered*
> *By God's almighty hand:*
> *He sends the snow in winter,*
> *The warmth to swell the grain,*
> *The breezes, and the sunshine,*
> *And soft, refreshing rain.*
> *All good gifts around us*
> *Are sent from heaven above;*
> *Then thank the Lord, oh, thank the Lord,*
> *For all His love.*
>
> *We thank Thee then, O Father,*
> *For all things bright and good,*
> *The seedtime and the harvest,*

Our life, our health, our food;
Accept the gifts we offer
For all Thy love imparts,
And what Thou most desirest—
Our humble, thankful hearts.

As the hymn ends, I continue my story:

"When farmers are growing their cops and raising their animals, it is very important that they remember how dependent they are on God for things like rain, sun, soil, seeds, everything that helps plants and animals to grow. Everything we have is a gift of God. Just as Paula's song says, we are to come to God with humble and thankful hearts.

"Unfortunately, there seems to have been something missing from the heart of Cain when he presented a gift to God. I think Cain was missing the attitude of gratitude. The story in Genesis tells us that Cain, after harvesting his fields, brought a gift of *some* grain to God. What would you think if I baked a large batch of brownies to bring to your party but decided at the last minute to leave most of them at home and bring just *some* of the brownies to your house? Maybe I bring only the burned ones and leave the perfect ones at home. You might think I was cheap and selfish. Cain brought *some* of his harvest to God; maybe as little as he thought he could get away with. Maybe Cain was feeling something other than thankful to God? Cain might have been saying to himself: 'I did all the work. No one is going to tell me to give a lot of my grain to God!' It looks like Cain forgot that everything we have is a gift of God. In fact, I think we live in a world today, where most people have forgotten this truth.

"Do you think God can tell if we are feeling thankful? I think that is what happened in the Cain and Abel story. God knew that Cain did not have an attitude of gratitude, but instead, a bad attitude. And Cain knew it. Cain knew that he had a *baditude*. And Cain got very angry when he realized that God also knew that Cain was really not thankful at all.

"This is where our story of the two brothers takes a very bad turn. God also knew that Abel was very thankful—and God was delighted with Abel's attitude of gratitude and his very generous gift. And that made Abel very happy, but it made Cain very jealous. Cain took his baditude and turned it into a *maditude*.

"Do you know what happened next? God noticed Cain's maditude and like any loving parent, God tried to have a good talk with his child Cain about this. God told Cain—and God loved Cain very much—that he had a choice to make. We all have many choices to make. Parents often talk to us about making good choices. And parents often remind us that if we make a bad choice one day, we can still make a good choice the next day. God reminded Cain that he could make a good choice.

"But Cain was too angry to listen to God. He was so angry that he took his brother Abel out into a field and—hit him! He hit him again, really hard. And Abel died out there in that field. Cain killed his brother Abel. He did not have to hurt his brother; he made a *choice* to hurt his brother.

"Mattie and I have been practicing a song that we are going to sing together right now."

We perform a song made popular by Mister Rogers and Daniel Tiger: "What Do You Do with the Mad that You Feel?"

Then, I continue the story: "I think it is amazing and wonderful that God, when talking to Cain about his anger, told Cain the same thing that Mr. Rogers and Daniel Tiger tell us in that song. We can choose what to do with our anger. We can choose to do what is right instead of what is wrong.

"I'm wondering if someone in our group is angry or maybe just tired of listening and talking? I think this would be a good time to play a game of freeze tag. Billy, would you be the leader?" We leave the garden. The kids go wild, running here and there. Most of the adults allow themselves to be tagged, but, despite their protests, the children keep unfreezing them. Billy keeps running around and can't freeze everyone, until some of the adults give up and sit down. Pretty soon, everyone else is sitting or frozen and Billy has won the game. We give Billy a round of applause.

Then Shari says, "We have something very important to talk about. Billy wants to share something with us."

Billy, who just moments before was enjoying the applause, now looks *uncomfortable*. Nevertheless, he comes forward and tells us about something that occurred the day before, after our meeting about the animals, when he experienced sadness that led him to feel mad as well. Billy shows us a knife his parents let him bring to camp. He tells us that he went into the woods and used his knife to cut bark off a birch tree.

Then he cut more bark off another tree. Billy told us that he threw the bark on the ground and yelled that he wanted the trees to die—but he didn't know why he wanted the trees to die. He was just feeling angry. Later that evening, Billy realized that he had done something bad. He had to tell someone, so he told his mom. Then they told his dad and the three of them went out to the woods to see how much damage had been done. Billy's dad said that three of the birch trees would probably die. Billy started to cry. His mom was crying too. Billy told his mom and dad how upset he had been after our program about animals dying. His emotion spilled over into hacking at these trees. They all agreed that Billy did the wrong thing with his emotions. For a while, they just stood around grieving for the trees—and the animals.

After relating this story, Billy tells us, "There were consequences. I had to give up my knife. I feel terrible about those trees." Then, he asks the group, "What should I do next?"

Shari says, "Think about that question. We will have a meeting tomorrow to share our ideas with Billy. Remember that some mistakes can be fixed; some can't. Sometimes the best we can do is ask for forgiveness and make a better choice the next time. But, the biggest thing all of us have to do when we have done something wrong is to remember that God always loves us. Also, we can love each other, no matter what."

Family Cluster, Day 4

We have a family meeting to share ideas with Billy, including forgiveness and appreciation for his honesty. At the end of our conversation, Billy decides to ask the camp's director if he can cut down the trees that will die and use the logs to make projects to sell at his church's mission fair at the end of the summer. That way the dying trees would not be wasted. (Later, the camp director agreed and that is what happened.)

We continue our day at Family Cluster camp with Genesis 4: 9-10, read by Blair, Billy's mom.

> *Then the LORD said to Cain, "Where is your brother Abel?" He said, "I do not know; am I my brother's keeper?" And the LORD said, "What have you done? Listen; your brother's blood is crying out to me from the ground!"*

I begin to explain these verses from the Bible. "God is a lot like our parents. Sometimes it seems like our parents have eyes in the back of their heads. God always knows when something is wrong and God, like our parents, wants to help. In this case, God still loves Cain and tries to have another conversation with him, just like loving parents do when their son or daughter makes a mistake. God wants Cain to accept responsibility for his terrible wrong. But Cain just pretends that he has no idea what has happened to his brother, Abel.

"Cain asks, 'Am I my brother's keeper?' Of course, he is! And Cain knows it. We all know that we are supposed to love our brothers and sisters and neighbors and friends, and even strangers and enemies. We are all part of God's family and we are created to be a family and to take care of each other."

Shari jumps up at that point and affirms that we are all brothers and sisters. "We all make mistakes," she says, "But when we do, the next right thing to do is to say something like this." She has the children jump up and form a line. Each holds a poster. Shari tells everyone that as each boy or girl turns their poster around, everyone is to shout the words on the poster. One by one, the posters turn:

> *It was my fault.*
> *I did it and I'm sorry.*
> *My bad. I'll try not to do that again.*
> *Please forgive me.*
> *I'm sorry I got so mad.*
> *I will help you fix what I broke.*
> *I forgot to make the right choice.*
> *I'm the one. I stole the cookie from the cookie jar!*

I ask Barry, who holds the final poster to explain it. He tells us about another camp he once attended. There, he learned a fun chant that they sometimes yelled out at the end of meals in the dining hall. It was a chant about blaming where no one accepts responsibility for the stolen cookie. Everyone blames everybody else. Then Barry and a couple of his friends introduce the chant.

Barry stole the cookie from the cookie jar.
Who, me?
Yes, you!
Couldn't be.
Then who?
Brenda stole the cookie from the cookie jar.
Who me?
Yes you ...

Blaming is a habit. Not accepting responsibility for our decisions and actions, is tragically common among adults and even entire countries. But we can change. We can say, "I did it. I'm sorry."

God tells us that we can master this habit, heal the addiction to irresponsibility and convert our character to candor. Especially, we can meet and know a merciful God who forgives, protects and loves us as an *unalterable*, fixed, attribute of the character of God.

Yet, as the Cain and Abel story announces with painful clarity, we can also choose not to tell the truth. "It wasn't me. It's not my fault that so many animals are dying. I didn't light the fires that are burning. The garbage in the oceans is not my garbage." Lying and denial are a curse of mankind on the creation.

Cain killed Abel. Tragically, his act of hatred and violence became the common history of all humanity up until a point in time when all of life on the planet Earth, as the stories in Genesis continue to tell us, was threatened.

What will happen next?

8

Humanity's Response to God's Grief

The days of our life are 70 years, or perhaps 80, if we are strong;
even then their span is only toil and trouble;
they are soon gone, and we fly away.
So teach us to count our days that we may gain a wise heart.
Psalm 90

In this new millennium, humanity is traveling on a perilous road. The vast majority of people seem unaware of the danger ahead or have chosen to keep this danger simmering on a far back burner of their lives.

Everyone gets to choose their path. However, in this chapter and the next, I am inviting you to dive deep into the confusion, chaos and global suffering found in the Noah saga and the Tower of Babel story. In those eras, humanity also seemed unaware of the coming catastrophes. I encourage you to feel the terrifying emotions appropriate to these stories—even as we all continue to rely on hope in God's incomprehensible love.

I don't believe these are children's stories, if we truly confront the fact that these accounts are meant to shake us to the core. The storyteller of the Noah saga weaves a dark and frightening tale of disobedience and destruction—death on an almost unimaginable scale. The storyteller raises demoralizing questions that are all too relevant today. God told Cain that sin was a devouring beast. What if Cain chooses, and keeps on choosing, to be devoured? God chose humankind to steward the creation. What if we choose to consume it?

God is love. The creation is good. But what happens within the heart of God when we are not good and are not loving? God birthed a creation, a cosmic adventure. Can this birth be aborted?

At the beginning of my own *lectio divina* of the Noah story, as I was preparing this book, I read the entire saga out loud to my wife. To a couple of verses, Kathy protested in shock, "That's not really from the Bible!?"

Then we got into the really tough stuff: God's anguish, God's grief as God knows that the beloved will not change, the decision God faces over whether to give up on humanity. Will God continue to be revealed in Genesis as Just Love? This is a quandary of universal proportion: Can God's purpose in speaking the universe into being be so utterly opposed by sinful humanity that God is forced to decide to un-create what God created? If we take the Noah saga seriously, we will face terribly difficult questions. God chose humankind to steward the creation. What if we choose to devour it?

We will see.

'The Wickedness of Humankind Was Great in the Earth'

That phrase is in verse 5 of Genesis chapter 6. As the Noah story begins, God sees that humanity is continually evil. The consequences of the angry decision of Cain to be devoured by sin has become the reality of the whole human race and there is nothing to mitigate our shared guilt.

How does God respond? With rage? No, the next verse says, "it grieved God." God can only grieve—suffer the pain of betrayal—weep for these beloved children who have chosen to say a habitual "No!" to their Creator God. We read that God was "sorry" that he had created the human ones. In God's heart, God grieved! Within that terrible sorrow God also gave up on the innocent animals and birds. Even the sighting of a pileated woodpecker could not soften God's pain.

Quickly we learn the devastating truth: God's shocking and frightening determination to obliterate all human beings, all animals, creeping things and birds. I resist allowing even a hint of this possibility to enter my consciousness. I am shocked. So many innocents will die; puppy dogs, salamanders and cardinals. The storyteller, speaking for God, will not let us misunderstand the nature of the problem. The problem is not embodied or disembodied evil. Humanity is the problem. The "devil" did not make us do it. Collectively, we are all responsible for the coming fate of the Earth. It appears in these opening verses of the Noah story that all is lost! The grand plan of God is about to be aborted.

Let that sink it.

Many will die very soon, and in the future millions and billions will never be born. God is about to shift the creation into reverse and take back the fifth and sixth "very good" days. No animals. No people. That is how the storyteller understands God's intent.

This is terrifying news! But, before you begin to think of God as a capricious character, capable of changing course and abandoning Love— let me remind you that, earlier in this book, Chapter 3, I explained how the way spirituality and science understand time has helped me to interpret the Noah saga in a new way. The storyteller had to tell the story sequentially, but in actual fact, God never changed God's mind. The trauma that God experiences in response to man's rejection is part of what it means to say that God is Love; always has been, always will be.

God Sees a Righteous Man

Back to the biblical story, then.

In the midst of God's vast grief—suddenly and unexpectedly—we learn that God has noticed Noah. It seems that God's grief has opened God's eyes to see that the very good creation still thrives in the life of Noah. All is not lost! Suffering love will not, cannot, abandon all the sons of Adam and the daughters of Eve, and animals great and small. God looks up from grief and remembers Noah.

God remembers, but there still is a cataclysmic future unfolding for most of the Earth community. There are consequences to all those millions of human choices against God. God cannot reverse those con-sequences. The flood is coming. Hope is so ridiculously fragile!

Just Love does what Just Love can do. And, many parents, who have had to watch children fall and not get up, fully understand God's pain and the limits of love's power.

The Great Flood

To really understand the Noah saga, you and I must *experience* some measure of God's colossal grief. The storyteller, in describing the flood that covered the Earth, repeats a poignant phrase, well designed to wring the sadness out of us.

Blotted out. Blotted out. Life is blotted out!

Life is strangled out of every living thing not on the ark with Noah and his family. The waters swelled on the Earth for 150 days. Life is blotted out.

We are supposed to be grieving over this story. We are supposed to be experiencing some portion of the suffering God knew when those who were created in the image of God betrayed the Divine love. We are supposed to feel regret and despair when we see the evidence of our continuing betrayal, children dying from hunger, creatures becoming extinct and the earth contaminated by greed. We are supposed to be suffering because suffering may lead to repentance and repentance to forgiveness and forgiveness to a new creation.

God Remembers Noah and the Flood Subsides

At last in chapter 8—a new beginning, a fresh start, the new creation.

> *But God remembered Noah and all the wild animals and all the domestic animals that were with him in the ark. And God made a wind blow over the earth, and the waters subsided. Then God said to Noah, 'Go out of the ark, you and your children, and your sons and your sons' wives with you. Bring out with you every living thing that is with you ... so that they may abound on the earth and be fruitful and multiply on the earth ...'*

The most important line here is the first one: "But God remembered Noah and all the wild animals and all the domestic animals that were with him in the ark."

The creation was saved from total destruction only because, in the midst of God's grief, God remembered Noah. We are reminded in Genesis 8:1 that everything depended on God remembering. Then, God announced that Just Love would not, could not, ever intend the total annihilation of humanity. In fact, I think it is fair to ask if God ever intended this.

However, the urgent question for us today is: What do *we* intend? Have we learned anything as we witnessed the grief of God and as it was revealed to us that our Loving God is also a suffering God?

The Covenant with Noah

Will we sign on to a new covenant with God?

> *Then Noah built an altar to the LORD.*
> *The LORD said in his heart,*
> *"I will never again curse the ground because of humankind ...*
> *As long as the earth endures,*
> *seedtime and harvest, cold and heat,*
> *summer and winter, day and night,*
> *shall not cease."*
> *God blessed Noah and his sons, and said to them,*
> *"Be fruitful and multiply and fill the earth ..."*

Once again, we have the calling God us gave in the beginning to fill the Earth with the goodness of God—to prosper, to be family, to care for each other and all of the creation. But have we signed this new covenant with our very lives?

Do you get the irony in this? In one sense the story announces that God and the creation and Noah and his family are back on course. But in fact, we don't sign on! The beloved children of God created in God's image still choose to rage, murder and destroy. We still can choose not to love God or our neighbors or the strangers all around us. To a perilous extent, humanity today continues to choose to be the warmongers, creation exterminators and inquisitors who oppress anyone who believes differently, loves differently or worships differently.

We have not signed the new covenant. In light of these stories we have just been reading: What hope is there? Here is the irony: If there is any hope to be found—it is not within the created world. On the other hand, we believe, hope is to be found everywhere because God is everywhere. Hope is not found in us—not in our technologies, politicians, economies or military machines. On the other hand, hope is found in us and in anything we do according to the purposes of God.

We are the ones, created in the image of God, who have still been gifted with the freedom and the power to say to God, "Yes!" However, as we continue choosing to behave counter to God's purposes, the question remains as it did in the days of Noah: What is God to do?

I had never before seen an answer to that question within the Noah saga. What did God do within the Noah story that God had never done before? What changed? The creation did not change. We see no evidence that human beings changed, not even a bit. So, what changed? Here is the only answer I can find in the Noah story: God reveals to humanity that God is a suffering God. The Noah story closes with God setting a rainbow in the sky as an eternal sign of God's faithfulness and undying love even in the midst of God's continual grief.

Then, how is this revelation going to change anything? Will humanity sign the new covenant? Not right away, that is certain. Through the rest of the Hebrew Scriptures, through thousands of years, the question remains open. We receive hundreds of other stories, poems, history lessons, songs, wisdom sayings and prophecies that continue to reveal more about this Divine Heart that suffers betrayal with bottomless grief as well as a profound longing for fellowship with God's beloved.

God's Compassion Despite Betrayals

Still, the story continues. The covenant remains on the table for humanity as a whole to consider—and for each and every person to weigh. Like Cain, every single human being has the choice, the freedom, the responsibility and the ability to decide for God.

The prophet Hosea makes the choice exceedingly clear when he, inspired by God, writes of his wife's repetitive betrayals and his longing to give her another chance. This remains God's longing also. In an agonizing back-and-forth narrative in chapter 9, Hosea describes God's eternal wrestling with humanity's continual betrayal:

When Israel was a child, I loved him, and out of Egypt I called my son.
The more I called them, the more they went from me; they kept sacrificing to the Baals, and offering incense to idols ...

Yet, God always concludes:

I will not execute my fierce anger ... for I am God and no mortal—the Holy One in your midst—and I will not come in wrath.

Hosea's powerful scene calls to mind Jesus's parable of the wayward or prodigal son. The father in that story is a personification of a God of unlimited and unconditional love. In both stories, if we are willing, we meet a God who waits and waits—and suffers and suffers—never giving up hope that the beloved one will choose to come home.

What difference does this make? Christians answer with one word: Jesus. We read the ancient Scriptures as pointing us toward Jesus.

From Isaiah 53:5: "He was wounded for our transgressions, crushed for our iniquities."

Then, from the New Testament in John 12:32: "And I, when I am lifted up from the earth, will draw all people to myself." And, Philippians 2:8: "Being found in human form, he humbled himself and became obedient to the point of death—even death on a cross."

We love because God first loved us. Jesus suffered and died for us. Is that suffering love a sufficient motivation for humanity to turn and be saved?

We will see.

9

Response-ability

Does not wisdom call, and does not understanding raise her voice?
On the heights, beside the way, at the crossroads she takes her stand;
Beside the gates in front of the town, at the
entrance of the portals she cries out:
"To you, O people, I call, and my cry is to all that live. O
simple ones, learn prudence; acquire intelligence, you
who lack it. Take my instruction instead of silver,
And knowledge rather than choice gold."
Proverbs 8: 1-5 and 10

Good news!

And it is very good news! Humanity has the ability to respond to God with a resounding, "Yes!" Whether this good news is announced in the Hebrew Scriptures, the New Testament—or any other source of wisdom—it is very good news to know that we have the capacity to choose to be on God's side. We can respond by loving God. We can respond by choosing good over evil. We can be one with God.

Sing out this old favorite song of faith, "Trust and Obey:"

When we walk with the Lord in the light of His Word,
What a glory He sheds on our way!
While we do His good will, He abides with us still,
And with all who will trust and obey.
Trust and obey, for there's no other way
To be happy in Jesus, but to trust and obey.

In the beginning, God commissioned and empowered us to steward the creation and to be fruitful and multiply and to love as God loved us. We were charged with responsibility but there's another deeper truth to this commission that we may forget: God also gives us the response-*ability* to put into practice God's ways and experience God's love.

History repeats itself, so let's look at the classic biblical story of people trying to say "No" to God.

Of course, we know that God always wants to bless the created ones— all of us around the world. However, in the Tower of Babel story, humans try to be like God and shift the glory to themselves. These creatures keep trying to find their own way into heaven—in this case by building of a great tower fashioned from the dust of the earth. Multitudes were building a city on the plains of Shinar, led by hotshots determined to make a name for themselves. Imagine the scene. Most likely, thousands of slave laborers were working themselves to death. Pushing them mercilessly were slave drivers cracking their whips. Among them were skilled craftsmen taking pride in their work: stone cutters, carvers, designers, architects and artists. Those craftsmen were doing fairly well, but not as well as a few powerful men shouting commands—working for the wealthy powerbrokers enjoying the opulence of the city. Can you imagine that scene? Perhaps you can recall scenes from Hollywood epics such as *The Ten Commandments*. So many are suffering! Only a few are glorifying themselves.

You don't have to look into the past to see these disparities. Simply look at the vast wealth gap today between the rich and poor. This is terrible news, isn't it? History is replete with examples of civilizations that have fallen because of the terrible suffering of masses engendered by an unconscionable distribution of wealth. Or, in 2020, you could simply look at front page headlines about the world's growing wealth gap.

So, let's turn to some good news—a story of people gathering in a city for an entirely different purpose.

First, two passages from Scripture promising the possibility of prosperous and blessed cities and communities:

> *The LORD will guide you continually, and satisfy your needs*
> *in parched places, and make your bones strong; and you shall*

*be like a watered garden, like a spring of water, whose waters
never fail.*
*Your ancient ruins shall be rebuilt; you shall raise up the foun-
dations of many generations; you shall be called the repairer of
the breach, the restorer of streets to live in.*

Isaiah 58:11-12

*Old men and old women shall again sit in the streets ... each
with staff in hand because of their great age. And the streets of
the city shall be full of boys and girls playing in its streets.*

Zechariah 5:4-5

Imagine a city like the ones described in these texts from the prophets
Isaiah and Zechariah. The folks living in this city have a great reputation.
They know how to build and fix things. They are making their neighborhood safe again so that abundant and joyful lives can be lived. From
all around, people visit just to walk around in this safe and beautiful
neighborhood. When you compliment these folks for the exquisite work
they have done, they quickly remind you how much everyone in the
neighborhood depends on their neighbors and how blessed they are to
live in this community. As you walk along the avenue, many residents
will wave to you from their front porches or chat with you, should you
have the time and interest for conversation that could build friendship.

I was a part of a community like that once for 10 years. I was not a
leader among the builders, restorers and fixers. I was a participant and
one among many who celebrated our neighborhood. And as pastor of
the brick church at the intersection of South Fountain and Miller, I was
a leader when it came to encouraging, inspiring and calling our social
and spiritual enterprise: "Good!"

In the 19th century, Springfield, Ohio, was a prosperous community,
and many of the wealthy built Victorian mansions on South Fountain
Avenue. During the Great Depression, magnificent homes were cut
up into small pieces and the neighborhood, with all of its stunning
architecture, decayed. Eventually crime, prostitution, drugs and deep
poverty took root in the community and one property after another was
abandoned.

When the South Fountain neighborhood was in its glory, one corner of the neighborhood was anchored by the First Baptist Church. But the church's building also was in decline and the congregation was faced with the decision—as were thousands of once-prosperous urban churches—to rebuild on site or rebuild in the suburbs. The church stayed in the city, but membership declined, and the neighborhood went from decay to ruin. All around the church was deterioration and devastation. In fact, the police occasionally used a room on the second floor of the church for surveillance of a crack house right behind the church. Some children who lived in that house were drawn to the safety and love of the church. Over time, these children and the rest of the neighborhood gave the church a renewed purpose.

The story of the South Fountain neighborhood could easily fill a book, but here is the main point: With the church's decision to stay in the neighborhood, plus the arrival of a few pioneers with a passion towards restoring old homes, the pulse of the community began to revive. The pulse quickened when a member of the church, Dr. Warren Copeland, became the mayor of Springfield and when the Rev. Dr. Wes Babian "recklessly," it was said, moved his family into the neighborhood. Add to that another courageous decision. The First Baptist congregation decided to mortgage its property to buy up most of the block on which the church sat, leading to the Rocking Horse Medical Center becoming the new occupant of most of that block. Many more families made bold decisions to take up residence. Under the leadership of Pastor Babian's son, Benjamin, the South Fountain Neighborhood Association was established. Among many other deeds of hope, hundreds of trees were planted.

When I became pastor of the First Baptist Church of Springfield in 2005, it was the easiest decision in the world for me to move into a grand old home across the street from the church and to eventually purchase a superlative and restored Victorian home a few blocks away. It was a privilege for me to invest my time serving on the board of the medical center and to become an active participant in the neighborhood associ-ation. It was a privilege to pastor a diverse congregation—all committed to the well-being of our community and the entire city.

Somewhere along the way, as the streets were becoming safer and the homes were being restored and the community was being transformed—we realized that the passage from Isaiah 58 really did describe our lives together. I realized that we had become "the restorer of streets to live in."

In both the South Fountain and the Tower of Babel stories we see people united for the purposes of building a city. But in the South Fountain story, many of us were aware that we came together for the purposes of God. The Bible presents various visions of the greatness of such livable cities.

This is Prophet Micah's vision:

> In days to come the mountain of the LORD's house shall be established as the highest of the mountains and shall be raised up above the hills. Peoples shall stream to it, and many nations shall come and say: 'Come, let us go up to the mountain of the LORD, to the house of the God of Jacob; that he may teach us his ways and that we may walk in his paths.'
>
> For out of Zion shall go forth instruction, and the word of the LORD from Jerusalem. He shall judge between many peoples, and shall arbitrate between strong nations far away; they shall beat their swords into plowshares, and their spears into pruning hooks; nation shall not lift up sword against nation, neither shall they learn war anymore; but they shall all sit under their own vines and under their own fig trees, and no one shall make them afraid; for the mouth of the LORD of hosts has spoken.
>
> *Micah 4:1-4*

What Kind of Communities Are We Building Today?

The key to our success in Springfield was our clarity of vision. We knew what we were striving towards at the First Baptist Church of Springfield and the South Fountain neighborhood. We were focused on beauty, restoring the brokenness of human lives, homes, neighborhood and city.

Around the world today there are millions of individuals and groups re-creating neighborhoods, saving lives, loving God and neighbor—and loving "enemies," as well. Every week, I discover more inspiring stories. While visiting my granddaughter Makenna just the other day, she told me that this was a special day at her school. It was called, believe it or not, "Global School Play Day." In schools all around the world, that day was a day for simply loving being alive. On the second page of the flyer sent home by the teacher was a list of all the curriculum objectives supported by a Global School Play Day. I couldn't hold back tears of joy. Children all over the world were discovering that every person matters—and that every child can make the world better for everyone. I know that many members of the Earth community today share the grief of God when witnessing the troubles and betrayals of humanity. We lament the abandonment of our calling to be stewards of the creation. We agonize over the countless children that are murdered and abused and neglected and grow up convinced that they are unlovable.

Yet, I have a daughter who by the time she was 9 years old understood a calling in life to provide a loving family to children: her own and others the community needs her to foster. My wife, Kathy, has always known that she has a calling to gardening. Has God revealed your true calling to you? I know that there is a shimmering movement of the Spirit of God whooshing its way all around this planet and throughout the whole universe. All you have to do is to say "Yes."

What was the sin that threatened to devour the city of Babel? There were many but the big one was pride—the kind of pride that utters pronouncements like, "Let us make our name great!" No mention of God. We will do this ourselves. If it suits us, we will destroy the habitat of whatever creature stands in our way. If we have to, we will exterminate native populations. Millions more may die for the sake of our greed.

As in the days of Noah, God grieves the choices we are making, but God also has promised that no act of God will destroy the creation. Unfortunately, we don't need God to touch off a flood that kills millions. As humans, we now have claimed the power to destroy anything we choose to obliterate. Physics, biology, chemistry and all manner of technologies have been used for good—and also to create weapons of mass destruction. Humanity's response to God these days seems to be: "This is our Earth, our country, our home and we will manage it any way we want." The question each of us faces today is: Have we joined the crowd on a death march toward Babel?

An early reader of this chapter, a pastor, sent me an answer to that question, saying that he has been preaching about this collective challenge. Then, he added his own observations about the world today. "If we look around the country and the world, we've had nonstop periods of rain and floods and catastrophes and can easily imagine other unstoppable tragedies that are coming our way. The stories in Genesis raise the question: Is human life so interconnected and human evil so potent that such evil can undo creation? The answer is yes. The impact of greed and negligence upon the planet has now reached a critical mass and catastrophe has begun. What, in God's name, will it take for us to repent and turn? I know this sounds apocalyptic, but for me it's literally true and is the clearest Word that comes to me when I ponder the stories of Noah and Babel. We could take comfort in the covenant with Noah. But that's too glib. The biblical covenants were not independent of sustained action by humans to destroy them. We can take the covenant with Noah as God's intent, but we cannot take it to mean it will be impervious to any measure of human folly. We are not invulnerable to the collective consequences of sin."

As I read David's response, I immediately thought of the great hymn:

Open my eyes that I may see, glimpses of truth You have for me; place in my hands the wonderful key, that shall unlock and set me free.

How do we open our eyes? In her book, *Mystical Hope*, the Rev. Cynthia Bourgeault, an Episcopal priest and retreat leader, explains that contemplative lifestyle and deep prayer are the spiritual practices that make this transformation possible. Such prayer immerses us in a sea of Just Love. That immersion is what sustains our lives, no matter what is happening in the world around us. She writes, "The problem, essentially, as we approach this important issue of contemplative prayer and compassionate action, is that we are working with an outgrown metaphysics. You could say we are still using a Newtonian theology in a quantum universe." She challenges us to look at the lives of models such as St. Francis, Dorothy Day, Mahatma Gandhi, Oscar Romero and Henri Nouwen.

Too often we would like to protest to God, "Too bad there's nothing I can do!" We need to realize that is a lie. We always have the ability to take action, in one form or another. Love is never powerless. The truth is that, as in the days of Noah and Babel, we have brought ourselves once again to the precipice of catastrophe. That may seem like more honesty than we can bear. Not so. The truth will set us free! We can repent and turn away from the sin that has broken our lives, our country and the entire planet Earth. We can act on behalf of the creation, on behalf of the future of our children and grandchildren. We can live in harmony, as one, with the creation.

10

The Cosmic Love Story

You cause the grass to grow for cattle, and plants for people to use,
To bring forth food from the earth, and wine to gladden the human heart.
The trees of the Lord are watered abundantly, the
cedars of Lebanon that he planted.
In them the birds build their nests; the stork has its home in the fir trees.
The high mountains are for the wild goats, the
rocks are a refuge for the coneys.
Psalm 104:15-16

I am a storyteller. I have written hundreds of stories for sermons, news-letters and talks with children. This book is full of illustrations, examples, accounts and tales. However, to fully understand how "storyteller" is not something I *do* but something I *am*, you would have to hang around me for a while. You would soon notice I answer most questions with a story filled with expressive detail. I tell stories because they are the spice to my life while, at the same time, stories invite others to enter my world. Stories help me to be open, vulnerable and establish significant friendships. I love to listen to the stories others tell for the same reasons.

Jesus shared crucial messages in stories called parables. Sacred Scriptures from all traditions include a myriad of stories. In attempts to explain and remember everything that really matters, religions, com-munities, cultures and nations tell stories. Stories, like songs, are easy to remember. Stories, with their power to convince people on an emotional level, can transform lives. For many believers whose encounters with God are the extraordinary-ordinary events of daily life, there is always a current grace-filled event to share in order to show forth the glory of God.

Today, a new creation story is emerging. It includes the creation of sentient beings like us but is much older than us. In fact, this new creation story tells us of a beginning some 13.77 billion years ago—a rather explosive event most often called the "Big Bang." It is a story of unimaginable scope covering the birth and death of stars, expansive forces and contracting forces that by some kind of miracle keep the universe expanding without flying apart or collapsing in on itself.

For me, this creation narrative—when merged with the Bible's insights on creation and God's eternal purpose—is a true, mind-bending and inspirational story. I certainly don't know the whole story yet. No one does. But I know it is a good story of a good creation in a good universe that is wholeheartedly on the side of love. This good universe is "on my side" as well, though not in the way human beings would often prefer. My personal preferences and needs are not the only things that matters in this universe.

Should this loving and unified creation story be widely known and well told, I believe that it would soften many of the rough roads that humanity will be traveling in the near future. I long, during whatever time is given to me, to keep learning and to keep telling this cosmic love story.

This great story addresses great questions like:

Where did we come from?

Why are we here?

What is the meaning of it all?

Do we live in a friendly universe?

With all the suffering and death in our world, how can anyone possibly believe, "God is Just Love?"

Can humanity turn and be saved?

How do we convince everyone that each one is my sister or brother?

I believe that it is the greatest love story ever in need of knowing and telling. And, the Christ story weaves its way through every thread of this love story.

I began learning the Bible's teachings on the creation very early in my childhood. I began hearing, learning and believing the teaching of science on creation a bit later. But it was not until the 1980s, when I read *The Universe Is A Green Dragon*, by Brian Swimme, that the staggering expanse of that story began to inspire me. I also discovered the writings of Thomas Berry about that same time. These—including *The Dream of the Earth* and *The Sacred Universe*—added clarity and depth to the great story, but also accomplished for me something of greater importance. Thomas Berry taught me that the core beliefs of my Christian faith and the deep insights of physics, astrophysics and cosmology told the same story. Tragically, however, I have learned during the past 20 months, while pursuing my research and writing project on spirituality and science, that the vast majority of people have never even heard it. Some know the story of beginnings and meanings from their spiritual tradition. Many know a small part of the evolutionary story taught by science. But the great universal love story that weaves spirituality and science into a tapestry of truth is not yet widely told.

Recently I asked a child if she would be willing to read three books that I often recommend to children and families. (Jennifer Morgan's three books can be found in the bibliography.) My intention was to discern what age children could best understand these stories. Soon, my proposal was enthusiastically embraced by the entire family—and turned into a multi-generational gathering of Mom, Dad and two children. I served as storyteller and started by talking about the Circle of Life, familiar to nearly everyone from the movie *The Lion King*. I spoke about that circle from the point of view of both Christian tradition and scientific knowledge. At the end, I asked each person to respond.

Heather, the mother, affirmed: "What I liked the most today is how you combined science and religion; the Bible's creation story and the science story like my husband teaches. I have never heard anyone even try to do that before. Your way of talking about it works. Really, it was so easy. The singularity had God's love in it. Then, the Big Bang? God's love goes everywhere. The stories are connected. Science and religion each tell the part of the story that the other can't. I had never thought of that before."

The great transformational story has gone by many names. I have heard it called "The Odyssey of Life," "The Immense Journey," "The Evolutionary Epic," "The Circle of Life," "The Great Story"—and "The

Cosmic Love Story." You can find an excellent summary of this story in *Thank GOD for Evolution, How the Marriage of Science and Religion Will Transform Your Life and Our World*, by evolutionary evangelist, the Rev. Michael Dowd. The great story describes the billions of years in the evolving history of creation. The details of the story keep on changing as science gains more knowledge of the history of the universe and religion matures in its knowledge of God. Each religion and culture can tell this story from their unique point of view. Michael Dowd, whose worldview was profoundly influenced by his deep friendship with Thomas Berry, believes that the adoption of this story as humanity's universal story will help unite humankind as one family. The Cosmic Love Story will remind us that we are all one. The fate of one is the fate of all. The story will guide us towards a sustainable future, even if it takes a long time to get there—even if the long journey includes suffering and destruction.

Berry, Dowd and many others also believe that each faith community on the planet can see its own stories as a part of The Great Story. That is exactly what I began to do, when I was invited to preach to a Christian congregation seeking to rebuild unity following a time of conflict. I knew that the church needed to be reminded of the ties that bound them together in Christian love. I decided to write an "echo reading," a repeat-after-me celebration of our shared faith.

This is the result.

The Cosmic Love Story

God Is.

God was before time & space.

God Is Just Love.

God is Creator.

The Creation is good.

God & creation are full of purpose.

Love is the purpose.

Love requires a beloved.

We are among the beloved.

We have trouble.

being loved and being loving.

Into the world Christ was sent.

Christ is "Immanuel."

Jesus is God with Us.

Jesus is Love.

Jesus loves me, this I know.

We can know this love.

We can be this love.

We can love God, neighbor and stranger.

We can be One.

We can trust God.

We can worship God.

We know, Jesus is Lord.

Christ is risen.

Death is defeated.

Life abundant is ours.

Now and forever more.

God is Just Love!

Introducing "The Cosmic Love Story," I told the people that if there was a statement that they could not faithfully echo, they could remain silent. In our first back-and-forth reading, I noticed 100% participation—however, little exuberance.

So, after a bit of encouragement we did the reading again. This time, I added to my voice the intensity of my conviction that this proclamation was both true and exhilarating. The congregation followed my lead—and you could feel the energy rising with the affirmation of each shared belief. The sanctuary was filled with joy. After the service, people let me know that they had experienced a fresh wind of harmony blowing through their church. It certainly was a hopeful step forward.

In all our spiritual traditions, and within all of our human communities, there are forces of division. The heartbreaking story of Abraham's sons, Isaac and Ishmael, is well known by Jews, Christians and Muslims. Many religiously motivated crimes have been committed down through the centuries. Peoples within nations, and among nations, have been decimated by an endless progression of secular wars as well. The human family desperately needs a shared story that binds us as one.

For this unity to be found by Christians—and for Christians then to respect other believers—I am convinced that we must focus our faith on Jesus as, first, the Universal Christ who has been present in the creation from the beginning, binding all things and all creatures together as one. Second, we must go back to the New Testament Gospels to meet Jesus of Nazareth again, as if for the first time. Third, we must deepen the spiritual practices that support ever deeper encounters with the Jesus of faith, who lives, as the old song says: "He lives within my heart!"

The Solid Rock of Hope

In my role as a pastor, teacher and spiritual guide, how can I present this expanded understanding of the Christ to Christians? Imagine that I have been asked to create a devotional reading on the subject of hope. I might write and share with folks a reading with the title, "The Solid Rock." If you are Protestant, you might already be humming the famous hymn:

> *My hope is built on nothing less*
> *Than Jesus' blood and righteousness ...*
> *On Christ the solid Rock, I stand,*
> *All other ground is sinking sand.*

Each time I sing that old song, I begin feeling the hope. The connection between the words and my soul is spontaneous and instantaneous. The same is true with other hymns, like "Amazing Grace" and "How Great Thou Art."

As I sing "The Solid Rock," I think: My hope is, indeed, built on nothing less than Jesus's blood and righteousness. But it is also built on something more. My hope is built on something more fundamental than the cross. Christ is the Alpha and the Omega, the beginning and the ending, the fullness, the wholeness, the complete story. The Christ! The Christ, one in Love with the Father and the Spirit before time began and after the ending of time. My hope is founded on the Christ in all the ways we know God in Christ, present, then, now and forever.

I am connecting with:

- Christ, God's Word bringing all things into being and holding all things together.
- Christ, shaping the universe, expressing God's Love, including an infinity of deaths and resurrections.
- Christ, redeeming the creation in the teaching, healing, peace-making, saving work of Jesus of Nazareth.
- Christ, present in the Jesus of faith who is as close to me as my breath.
- Christ, who came, is among us and comes again.

My hope is built on nothing less than Christ, the fullness of God. Not just on one of the ways the Christ guides, sustains, saves. All the ways.

This affirmation of the Universal Christ also opens the door to affirming the efforts of other seekers after truth from other spiritual traditions. They also can build unity within their traditions and deepen conversations with other believers. Contrary to popular wisdom, those two goals are not mutually exclusive. In fact, they can and must happen simultaneously, because deep in the soul of every faith tradition is the knowledge that we are all one, or hope is lost. God is Just Love, or we are all lost.

I Am Made of Stardust

We need to translate the Cosmic Love Story for the purpose of sharing it with children. Of course, that is more than a bit problematic since children come in various ages and understand an immense variety of languages. The good news is that this work of translation is not solely in my hands. Maybe it is your work, too.

After the warm encouragement of the family I described above from Hide-A-Way Hills, I was determined to work on the telling of the story to children around Morgan's age, which is 9. I decided to write the story, again, in the form of an echo reading. The reading would be written with words and ideas Morgan could understand. She would read each line and the rest of us would energetically respond by repeating her declarations. This is what I sent to her so she could practice.

God is Just Love!
God's love made the stars.
I am made of Stardust.
God's love is in me!

God is Just Love!
God's love made everything.
Everything, everyone, is Stardust.
God's love is everywhere.

God is one!
I am one with God.
We are one with God.
Everyone, everything, is one.

I love my neighbor as myself.
We are one. My neighbor is myself.
We are one with everyone.
We are one with everything.
Animals, plants, air, water,
Always one. Always together. Never alone.

I am Stardust.

I am loved.

I am love.

We are Stardust.

We are loved.

We are love.

We are one.

Shout it!

We are love.

God is Just Love.

So be it!

Be it!

So be it!

Amen!

Morgan was ready when her family I got together the next time. She read her part of the story skillfully and enthusiastically. I knew that we were on the track of a winner—but this was only a beginning.

Morgan, speaking carefully, not wanting to hurt my feelings, told me, "I can do better for kids my age."

Yes, I suspect she can. Maybe she will. Maybe you will also. This story needs a planet full of writers and tellers from all spiritual traditions if it is to truly become The Cosmic Love Story that binds all of us together.

11

Telling the Truth to Our Children

O my people, hear my teaching;
listen to the words of my mouth.
I will open my mouth telling stories;
I will utter dark and hidden things from of old,
told to us by our fathers and mothers.
We will not hide these things from our children;
we will tell our children
the praiseworthy deeds of the LORD, the power of God,
and the wonders God has done.
Psalm 78:1-4

Psalm 78 addresses a fearsome issue. Our children are approaching a future that is certain to bring them face to face with grave perils related to resource depletion, environmental degradation and climate chaos. What do we tell our children?

There are dark and hidden things in our culture, in our families, in ourselves. How much do we hide from our children? On the other hand, there are the wonders all around us. Do we have the capacity, experience and personal relationship with God that empowers us to tell our children of the power of God's presence in the world, in our lives? Are we able to nurture in them amazement when encountering the wonders of God?

Meet Maxton. He is my 4-year-old grandson. Maxton is among the most emotionally sensitive and loving children I know. For example, he easily falls in love with the vulnerable foster brothers and sisters that come and go within his family. He embraces them with joy, and quickly becomes a caregiver (as with two 1-year-old twin girls who are currently his sisters). He weeps when they depart—and within a few days opens his heart again.

On a Monday morning this past summer, my wife, Kathy, and I took Maxton and his sister Makenna to the zoo. Dad was at work. Mom was in South Africa on a mission trip. Our mission that day was to give our two grands undivided attention and affection in this time of missing Mommy. We were doing pretty well—until we came to the African section.

Makenna saw the map at the entrance. Pointing to South Africa she exploded, "That's where Mommy is!"

Maxton began to lose it. Tears formed.

Kathy saved the day by announcing, "We will take a picture of you by the map of Africa and send it to Mommy. Right now!" We wound up sending a video with the message that we missed Mommy, were still having fun and hoped Mommy had already found new friends in South Africa to serve and to love. I wish you could have seen our little movie. Makenna was so funny! Even Maxton began laughing at her video antics.

We were back on mission. After a camel ride, a rest stop with lots of snacks restored our energy. On to Asia. Our grands love the snakes in Asia. They have been taught by their cousin Alison, who keeps snakes as pets, to celebrate these too-often-maligned creatures. There we were, being held in the gaze of a king cobra. Suddenly, I broke away from this stare when I realized that Makenna and Maxton were—gone!

I should have known. They don't do a lot of "screen time" in their family so an animal video had attracted them like moths to light. The film soon ended, but not their attention. My suggestion that we move on was ignored, as if I had not spoken a word. Maxton and Makenna were intent on watching the video, again.

Can't beat 'em? Join 'em! Soon enough, all of us were listening and watching with rapt attention as the narrator painted a stark picture of humanity's cruelty towards animals. I felt sick. I could only imagine what Makenna and Maxton were feeling. Do I need to protect them? Drag them away? Before I could figure things out, the video ended. Maxton bolted from his seat and began passionately, in detail, informing us of what cruel men do to tigers, elephants and other creatures great and small.

"Maxton," I responded with reverence and resolve, "When we get back to the car, we can talk about what we can do to protect the animals." That is exactly the conversation we had all the way home; and again, later in the evening. A couple of weeks later, with Mom safely back from South Africa and the family gathered to celebrate two birthdays, Maxton was given the honor of leading the family prayer before dinner. In his prayer, he declared, "When I grow up, I will be a scientist and save the animals."

Oh my! This made me rethink who can handle the "dark and hidden things" of humanity's abuse of creatures and creation. How much of the darkness from which we adults try to protect our children is exactly the knowledge they must have in order to live and love within the coming perils?

In 1998, my daughter Lauren was 14 years old. I had been invited by Lazaro Gonzales, the president of a Baptist seminary in Mexico City, to lead a conference on missions. Lauren traveled with me. She came prepared to teach children in villages we would be visiting after the conference. Very early one morning we headed out of the city. On the outskirts of Mexico City, we passed a garbage dump. I had passed by this same dump in 1971. Then it was just a dump, with a few garbage pickers meandering through the piles. But in 1998 it was home to thousands of children. Such desperate, life-destroying, poverty is on the rise in many countries around the world. There are now plenty of videos online that show these real-life scenes, but would you show such videos to your children? Do they need to be exposed to such dark and hidden things? At what age? In what ways?

That exposure to an extremity of human suffering cemented a decision that Lauren told me about only recently. A commitment, a life mission, had been percolating in her heart, soul and mind. Passing by that garbage dump, passing by those children already busy picking through the garbage, Lauren then and there *knew* that the purpose of her life was to provide a loving home to children. Today she, her husband, Jeff, and their two birth children are a foster family. Children, coming in and going out, know they are loved. Just loved. Period.

Lauren keeps learning and growing in her role as a professional parent. During our visit to the zoo that I described above, Lauren was in South Africa with a team from her church helping a community to grow a foster-care/adoption system that includes caring for special needs children.

Of course, I am proud of her. I'm also thankful that, as parents of young children ourselves, the idea of protecting our children from truth and reality was never high on our agenda. The unfolding of love in their worlds created contexts wherein they could decide for themselves what and when they were ready to see, to know, to process. Our calling was to avoid getting in their way or God's way.

Parents, grandparent, teachers, right now, consider making a promise like this: "We promise that we will not hide afflictions and fearsome possibilities from our children. Instead, when they come face to face with painful reality and dark circumstance, we promise to be Just Love—to be there holding, listening, sharing our experience and wisdom as needed. We promise that love, not fear, will be the guiding word of our hearts and our homes and our relationships."

Are you able to make such a promise? The only way you and I can make such a promise to our children—to their future on earth and in heaven—is if we are growing emotionally and spiritually toward hope and love. Hope that sustains the lives of our children cannot be founded on the illusion that we can control the circumstances of their lives, that everything will be fine, or that we can fix the predicaments humanity faces.

Things I Can Change—and Those I Cannot

Consider the difference between problems to be solved and predicaments that must be honestly faced. Most of us have heard the classic prayer:

> *God, grant me the serenity*
> *To accept the things I cannot change;*
> *Courage to change the things I can;*
> *and wisdom to know the difference.*

That challenge is a lot harder than it sounds!

Kathy and I recently decided that owning just one car that averages over 30 miles per gallon would significantly reduce our budget for transportation and our carbon footprint. Problem solved. Maybe we will use the savings to "go solar" and reduce our dependence on the electrical grid. Another problem solved. There is, however, no solution to the predicament that our planetary sources of cheap non-renewable fuels—oil, gas, coal—are being depleted. Treating this predicament as a problem to be solved with new technologies inevitably creates new problems that deepen our predicament. I have only recently abandoned my belief that technology is a godlike force that will always save us. You can easily recall all the promises we have heard over the past century. Nuclear power will save us. Solar power will save us. Engineering marvels and scientific geniuses will save us. Even though I was convinced for many years that there are limits to growth, I often found myself putting my hope in the belief that human ingenuity can solve all problems. After my immersion in this research for a couple of years, however, I have given up my faith in unending economic progress through the saving power of the latest technologies.

On the other hand, time and time again, God has been planting seeds of hope within my heart that I then strive to plant in the lives of others. God is Just Love. God guides. We can listen and follow. This really works! It's a perfect time to begin your own journey towards Just Love.

What do we tell our children about all of this? On an initial hearing of Psalm 78, which opens this chapter, it seems reasonable to assume that telling our children the praiseworthy deeds of the Lord is much easier than telling them of dark and the hidden things. However, that depends on your operational image of God. When the going gets tough, do you trust that the love of God will remain an ever-present force?

It took me many years to reach that point. I was in my late 30s before I confronted the truth that my own operational image of God was that, when circumstances got really bad, God would be absent. I was on my own. No help was forthcoming. The dreadful feeling that defined my life was a fear of abandonment. The root of that fear was my childhood experience of my father disappearing repeatedly because of a deadly condition. More than once, he went off to the hospital with my mother at his side to die. My brothers and I were sent to stay with grandparents. As my parents struggled with this health crisis, they must have been exhausted with fright. Given the emotional boundaries in the mid-1950s, there was little attention paid to helping me process my terrors. I only came to fully face them many years later when they erupted in my life in the form of endless nights of weeping too deep for words. Yet, that eruption of pain from the past was the beginning of a new future wherein I eventually came to know, "God is Just Love."

On the day you *know* that God is Just Love you will stop wishing, hoping, praying, pleading, or crying out, "God, *do* something!" You will know that God is always doing everything that Love can do. You, too, will then want to do everything that love can do to transform the world. You will also know that you can act to empower your children to know God's present love.

When the Presence of God Surprises Us

As a pastor and spiritual director, I know the huge obstacles that lay between most of us and that kind of deep faith that God loves us unconditionally. For many years, I have sat with men and women who came to tell their stories honestly—stories that sometimes include terrible experiences and horrendous family secrets. I am always amazed at how these adults have survived, often courageously and against all odds. Often, the people telling me these stories say they are convinced that a loving God would never have tolerated such trauma.

As I listen, I grieve with them. Eventually, the moment arrives when I respond with questions like:

- How did you survive?
- What did you hold on to?
- With all that pain, how did you get through to tomorrow?

I have heard answers like:

- I lay in bed crying, holding onto my doll. Her name was Susie. I cried again and again, "At least you love me Susie."
- My kitty, Persimmon. We curled up in a corner and we held on to each other. I petted, she purred.

- Mrs. Tindley. She seemed to know. I walked by her house coming home from school. She always smiled and waved and many days we had cookies together.
- I would pretend that Miss Jane, from TV's *Ding Dong School,* was my mother. I drew pictures for her. She always loved them; but I hid them from my parents.
- My bed was covered with stuffed animals. My favorite was Floppy Ears; one Christmas my Sunday school teacher gave him to me. I was not alone at night and less afraid.
- One summer, my aunt, who lived far away, came for a visit. She gave me a book, *Owly.* It's tattered, but I still have that book. She hugged me and said that she had more hugs for me than there were stars in the sky.
- My dog, Bison, he looked like a buffalo. He always knew when I needed a friend. Wherever I hid, Bison found me. He died when I was 17. I cried for days.

A doll named Susie? A kitty named Persimmon? A book called *Owly*? The list goes on and on. There was something that each child held tight. Each doll, pet, book, person, was how God's presence was experienced at the time. When adults, who must learn to care for their inner wounded children, remember and make the connection—they discover a reason for considering that God may not have been absent, uncaring, or even raging, as a human father had been experienced. It becomes possible for the adult to give God another chance and convince the wounded child that she/he will be safe. Suddenly it becomes possible for that adult to be Just Love to a vulnerable child.

The point is simply this: You and I cannot convincingly tell our children the stories of "the praiseworthy deeds of the LORD, the power of God and the wonders God has done" unless the stories jive with our own life stories. We can never trust an image of God we see as absent, angry, judgmental, aloof, uncaring, violent or legalistic. In fact, maybe the most damaging image of God in a time of crisis is the assumption that God is in control of everything and, thus, has caused this catastrophe and is responsible for suffering. In this image of God, devastation is our just deserts. God is the great punisher and we have run out of time.

That's why I urge people not to waste another minute. The time is now to seek Truth—God as love and only love. That's when people ask me: Where do I start?

Often, I refer them to a book, like Philip Yancey's *Disappointment with God*, which is terrific for helping readers to re-form their destructive images of God. I also like to give copies of Sarah Young's *Jesus Calling*. She speaks to the reader as the voice of God, helping us to feel God up close and personal. She must personally know this God of love very well to write this way.

Nearly always I encourage people to find a safe place to connect with others on the journey. I often say things like:

- There is a place, a community, where you can share your struggle to trust God, to really know God as Just Love. Look for that place until you find it.
- Stay away from people, including many Christians, who feel they are empowered to judge you.
- Just start. Decide that knowing God's love and being love to others is the foremost priority of your life.
- Be honest about your idols and tell them to, "Get out!"
- Tell God, "Come on in!" Once you invite God into your life, one good next step is to pay attention to the words of the Lord that are always coming your way, like invisible radio waves that surround you.
- Become available to God by spending time in creation, in silence, in the Bible or a devotional book and especially in prayer.

In spiritual-life retreats, I often share a devotional practice "Listening to God in Scripture" through four steps:

1. In reverence, take the Bible in your hands. Ask God to be present in your reading and in your day.
2. Read and listen for 10 minutes. Notice when a word or phrase captures your attention.
3. Write that word down. Take it with you into your day. Notice when that word of God connects to your life experience.
4. Thank God, at the end of the day, for being with you.

People who practice this discipline for many days begin to notice God's presence in the ordinary events of life. Their relationships with God begins to grow. Remember that God speaks every language, even the language of your "clumsy attempts." Keep your antennas up.

Writing Your Own Prayer of Remembrance and Thanksgiving

Consider writing a prayer of remembrance and thanksgiving, like the one I am about to write:

> *I thank you, God of my past, present and future. I thank you that I will never be alone; that you will never run out of love for me. Years ago, you were loving me when Mrs. Sunny was my Sunday school teacher and made church fun.*

> *You were loving me when my new friend shared an hour of ice water and conversation on my porch. He helped me to feel included.*

> *You, my God of unconditional love, are the solid ground on which I stand, no matter what is shaking around me.*

> *You protected me years back when the wolves of criticism and judgment were nipping at my heels.*

> *So it is that right now, as I pause to pray in the middle of tackling my to-do list of 99 items, I thank you again and say, "God of love, I love you."*

> *I say "Yes!" to you as the voice of love I long to follow.*

> *Later today or tomorrow, I may forget to stop in the middle of all my doings. Yes, I probably will, sometime soon, forget to remember you. Even then, you will remember me. When I return, your arms will be open and I will not be made to feel like a failure.*

> *Right now, I give you the praise and gratitude that brings joy to your heart, because right now I remember. I remember love. Right now, I promise to be your love to Myron who has a*

broken heart and John who is so lost that he needs me to find him before he can stop hiding from you.

Right now, I am looking for you in the quiet of my life when your love is shining forth from the created world of trees, breeze, fields and harvest yields.

God of my past, present and future, Your love is everywhere and always with me and Your forgiveness is from beginning to the end. You are my hope. It is so!

Amen.

That's my prayer. What's yours?

Taking Practical Steps

Ultimately, there are many practical steps families can take to move closer to God as Just Love.

One of the most powerful experiences I found as a pastor through 40 years of ministry was to invite families to participate in short-term mission trips. Earlier in this book, you met Willow DiLuzio, a microbiologist, who spent a life-changing week with her 12-year-old daughter serving hurricane victims in Puerto Rico. You don't have to travel that far. You could serve meals with your children at one of the missions in America's inner-city neighborhoods. See with your children how you can make this a better world. Show them that faith, hope and love can be formed and nurtured in suffering communities everywhere. Open their eyes. Open your eyes.

Trust your children. You cannot protect them from the suffering in your life. They will feel it. They will be wounded by that pain or blessed by it. Let them in and prepare to be surprised by their insight and love. They need to know how much you trust God. Be real. Be love. Give them a chance to be love for you.

Watch a movie together. Kathy and I enjoyed a rather unusual comedy, *What We Did on Our Holiday* (2014). Major themes in the film include the consequences of lying to our children, the capacity of children to adjust to difficult truth and the fact that wounded human beings can experience healing and can become love. Depending on your children's ages, you might want to preview the film before inviting your children to watch it with you. The film has some rough language, raw emotion, deep brokenness—and superb examples of tragically immature adult behavior. Your children will love that part! It will give you a chance to confess, to acknowledge your imperfection, to give them permission to be imperfect without fear of being rejected.

Create new opportunities with your children to stand by your side and experience the truth of this world. It is crucial that something or someone shine a penetrating light on our lives and our times. We cannot tell the children the truth if we ourselves our denying the truth and desperately dodging responsibility for the brokenness of our lives and our world.

Let's all do more to help our children find hope and be love in the midst of the suffering in our world and as we move into a perilous future.

12

Seeds of Hope for Children's Souls

Listen, listen to the thunder of his voice and the
rumbling that comes from his mouth.
"Hear this, O Job; stop and consider the wondrous works of God."
Job 18: 2, 14

What is the source of hope that always sustains?

Consider the story of Job. Remember what he lost? Everything.

Job's suffering was apocalyptic. First his property, then family, health, peace and certainty of God's care. Then came the assaults of supposed friends who blamed him and maimed his integrity and faith. All that was left was destitution.

How was hope restored? In his suffering, Job cried out to God. Job felt the extremity of his pain and let it all hang out. He vehemently protested his innocence. Job's raging dispute was immediately followed by an extraordinary encounter with God. God spoke to Job out of a tornado—a whirlwind of climate-chaos ferocity. The reality of such a storm would not abide denial.

God said nothing comforting, reassuring or affirming. God said nothing to convince Job that his lot in life would ever improve. But, within the storm, Job experienced the presence of God: ultimate reality, Love in the guise of a whirlwind of words. What Job needed to recover his hope was presence, first-person knowing that God was still God of the universe, God of everything: Job's God.

That is the source of our hope: a relationship with God, Just Love; God who never abandons, despite the deepest loss.

Is it possible that we can help the children we love to stand on such a sure foundation of hope?

Teach the Children to Sing

On Thanksgiving Day 1986, I was not feeling thankful. In fact, I was in the midst of a deep crisis, feeling enveloped in a thick fog. That's when my brother John invited me to go for a walk. I accepted. I followed him down toward the pond.

Here's how John began the conversation:

John: *Ken, do you remember the songs we used to sing in vacation Bible school?*

Ken: *(I began to smile.) Do you mean like, "Do Lord, O Do Lord, O do remember me, O Lordie!"*

John: *Dad taught us that song. Another one was, "The Lord Knows the Way Through the Wilderness."*

Ken: *Yes, I remember.*

We began to sing:

The Lord knows the way through the wilderness,
all I have to do is follow.
The Lord knows the way through the wilderness
all I have to do is follow.
Strength for the day is mine on the way,
and all I need for the 'morrow.
The Lord knows the way through the wilderness,
all I have to do is follow.

John: Just keep singing. Don't stop singing.

So, I kept singing, all the way around the pond and back up to the house—that is, singing through my tears. During that walk with my brother, I was not feeling so alone. John seemed to know something about my path of hopelessness. He walked beside me. The darkness faded a bit. We reentered Mom's house and enough light was shining in and around me that I was able to enjoy Thanksgiving dinner with our family.

Of course, the shadowy darkness would return and settle in around me again, but I kept singing. The memory of learning the song as a 6-year-old—plus the memory of singing it almost every Sunday in Mrs. Sunny's Sunday school class—helped to keep me moving forward, one day at a time.

So, my first counsel is: Don't forget the song. Don't forget to sing. Don't forget to teach your children to sing. Teach them when they are very young so the songs can take root in their hearts, never to be forgotten.

As my brother John reminded me back on that Thanksgiving Day, Dad taught us to sing, "The Lord Knows the Way Through the Wilderness." When did Dad teach us the song? Exactly when he was being led across the wilderness, through the valley of the shadow of death, traveling again and again to a veteran's hospital in Buffalo, New York—again and again expecting to die. He did not die, not then, and he kept teaching us to sing. The way I remember the story is that, in the summer of 1955, he was miraculously healed. Dad sat across the desk from his doctor and was told about a new surgical procedure. He would be the first one to have it at that hospital.

Following that long ordeal, Dad took John, Jim and me to Pathfinder Lodge in Cooperstown, New York, for family camp. Mom stayed home to care for 18-month-old Terry, and because she was nine months pregnant with Tom. Dad and his sons had a terrific time. We won the treasure hunt, got lost in a torrential downpour and learned the song, "Little Cabin in the Woods," with motions for every line.

> *Little cabin in the woods.*
> *Little man by the window stood.*
> *Saw a rabbit hopping by.*
> *Knocking at the door.*
> *"Help me, help me, help me," he cried*
> *"Er the hunter shoot you dead."*
> *"Little rabbit come inside.*
> *Safely you'll abide."*

That song eventually became a theme song of our family reunions and John, the eldest brother, was called upon to lead us in singing, year after year. "Help me! Help me! Help me!" cried the little rabbit in the song, year after year.

Many years later, John suffered a stroke; then another. He died. So tragic. At John's memorial service, nephew Chris inherited the role of song leader. Chris led us in the tale of remembrance, all the verses of "Little Cabin in the Woods." With each succeeding verse we remembered, ever more deeply, how much we loved John. Lots of tears, yet nothing but joy. Songs remind us of messages but even more they remind us of love and often are our life-saving connection to hope. John died—but the rabbit was and always will be saved, as long as we remember to sing the song.

Teach the children to sing songs of life, hope and love. They won't forget.

Teach the Children to See

I know death is followed by resurrection. Destruction is followed by construction. Termination begets creation. An end is a beginning.

How do I pass this knowledge on to the children? The evidence is all around us. Recently, during a walk in the woods near our home, I pointed out to my granddaughter Makenna the green leaves on a tree. A few were beginning to change color. We talked about leaves falling and dying. I asked her if the leaves would stay dead. Makenna was sure they would. But as we dug up layers of dead leaves, we began to see that they were becoming part of the soil, black dirt. Here's how our conversation turned:

> Me: What grows in black dirt? What would happen if we put an acorn in that dirt?
>
> Makenna: It would grow a new tree.
>
> Me: That's how the leaves that die, and fall to the ground, live again. Everything that is alive dies and then lives again. Have you ever heard a leaf complain that it must die and fall to the ground?
>
> Makenna: Leaves can't talk!

Me: Maybe we also can keep the silence, like the leaves. Maybe they know a secret we don't know. They give life to the future. It is the same for you and me.

For some time, I have been working on a children's book with the title, *What's Inside an Apple Seed?* I'm going to use the deer and raccoons that go out for dinner in our back yard as characters in my book. Kathy feeds them apples and corn. She has this theory that, if she feeds them well in the back yard, they will not eat her plants in the front yard. The story may open with a baby deer, Spot, trying to eat a big apple, but half of the apple falls to the ground. Spot wants to know what the little brown things are inside the apple. The story could end with a wise raccoon, Rascal, teaching Spot that love is inside the seed—and inside everything else, including Spot, you and me.

Can you think of other ways to teach your children that love is everywhere and that even death is one of the ways love does its work?

Teach the Children to Pray

I cannot overemphasize the importance of teaching our children to be thankful people. An attitude of gratitude is, in my experience, the easiest way to stay connected to the Giver of all good and perfect gifts. Take a few moments in the midst of a difficult day to notice the blessings that surround you. If you can't think of anything else, there is always the air you breathe and the gravity that never lets you go. There was a moment yesterday when I was frustrated by the unfairness of life. I noticed a shadow I had allowed to darken my spirits. Instead of dwelling there, I turned my thoughts to the life-sustaining love I experienced that morning in a conversation with Kathy. I held onto that feeling of gratitude for a few moments. I realized, once again, how thankful I am that unmerited grace abounds in my life.

Before we begin to explore some ways we can guide the children we love toward lives of gratitude, could we consider a collective prayer of confession?

Could you acknowledge with me that our lives within a materialistic culture continually deceive us into thinking that what

we have is ours by right, achievement, merit, rather than grace? That we and our children are severely tempted toward an attitude of entitlement rather than thanksgiving? That our extravagant lifestyles have damaged the planet, have left other human beings in the dust of poverty and have cost the future that our children will inherit precious resources?
God in your mercy, forgive us.

As long as I can remember, our family's Thanksgiving celebration has included the ritual, common to many families, of going around the table with the slightly forced expectation that everyone will share what they were especially thankful for that year. Generally, the children are creative. Their answers provoke laughter and appreciation. The adults? You sometimes get the feeling that we are embarrassed to go deep, to expose ourselves, to be authentic. Except one year, after we had all had our not-too-exuberant turns, Elaina, age 9, called out with excitement, "Let's do it again."

"Good job, Elaina!" I cried.

When a child leads like that, it is pretty much incumbent on the adults to follow. Our answers became a bit more interesting, personal, even surprising.

In the last few years, with the strong support of the children, we expanded our ritual. We gather before the feast begins, thus taking out of play any concern that the food will get cold. We include a couple of Thanksgiving songs that I lead on guitar, like:

Thank you Lord for giving us love.
Thank you Lord for giving us love.
Thank you Lord for giving us love.
Right where we are.

Alleluia, praise the Lord.
Alleluia, praise the Lord.
Alleluia, praise the Lord
Right where we are!

To form the following verses in the song, someone shouts out another word to insert for "love"—and we're off into another thankful verse.

The kids get a kick out of trying to trick me with phrases that don't fit the tune, like, "Mrs. Black is my third-grade teacher." I've learned to play and sing, "Thank you Lord for—" Then, I stop playing the guitar and emphasize every word: "—giving Sara Mrs. Black as her third-grade teacher."

This year, after the singing and laughing, I asked our teenage grand-daughter, Alison, to share a Thanksgiving prayer from the Mohawk Nation. I told our family that my hope was that this prayer would shift our thoughts and behaviors away from the way our culture treats the Earth, as a trash heap, as a thing, as resources that we may use and abuse at will. I invited them to consider, and later learn more about, the way native peoples all over the world have always seen and loved the creation.

At the end of the Native American prayer, I told this story:

You all know that where Kathy and I lived in Hancock, there were 75 black walnut trees and about 1,000 spruce trees planted by my mom and dad. I decided to harvest some of the trees. The trees were my dad's gift to the future, to all of you grandchildren, and I wanted to make sure that all of you benefited from that gift. When I began cutting down the trees, I didn't know a lot about using chainsaws. Sometimes I was in a hurry and got careless. I crushed a new chainsaw when a black walnut tree fell on it. Not so good. But there was this one tree, a very tall cherry tree growing right by the river. I knew the lumber from that tree would be very valuable. Two friends were with me. We decided to harvest this tree the right way, the Native American way. So, we had a ceremony before cutting the cherry tree down. We made an offering of thanks-giving to the tree by sprinkling cornmeal all around the tree and promising to use the wood wisely. Then we shared a lot of opinions about how to cut down this tree. Finally, my friend Micah came up with a plan—and it worked perfectly. You can see some of the wood from that tree as the tabletop in our din-ing room. There still are hundreds of board-feet of lumber from

that tree in my woodworking shop, in Micah's woodworking
shop and in Uncle Matt's shop. I will always be grateful to that
cherry tree for sharing its life with us.

Indigenous cultures all over the world, from the beginnings of human life on this planet, always knew that the creation was sacred, that every aspect of creation, the animals, plants, trees, water, soil, seeds—everything—is a gift of the Creator. When we live in harmony with the creation, the gifts of God will take care of us, and we will take care of them.

In native cultures, thanksgiving was a way of life. Sadly, we have been destroying creation at a faster and faster pace since the beginning of the industrial age. Now the creation is fighting back. We are living in a time of terrible tragedy. We cannot fix everything that has gone wrong, but we can enrich the lives of the children we love by teaching them to be thankful people who know that within the circle of life, the only gifts we ever keep are those we give away.

When Kathy and I gather with our immediate family, currently four children, four spouses and 11 grandchildren, table grace is always an outside-anyone's-control happening. Sometimes the children compete for the privilege and sometimes we just wait for an answer to the question, "Who wants to lead grace?" Maxton, age 4, sometimes just shouts out the Superman Grace, his fist flashing towards the sky, "Thank you God for giving us food!"

We also like to sing the Johnny Appleseed prayer:

O, the Lord is good to me,
And so I thank the Lord
For giving me the things I need,
The sun and the rain and the apple seed.
The Lord is good to me.
Amen! Amen! Amen!

Almost always there is someone, just as likely one of the children, who has something quite serious on their mind and adds a deep thought to our ritual. From Elaina's heart, "Today we miss Kasey who is off serving our country. Keep her safe." Or, from Makenna's spirit, "God, keep the animals in Africa safe from the hunters." Sometimes, after a child prays, the adults just look around at each other with expressions of wonderment: Where did these kids come from?

The answer is obvious: They came from us. By example, we taught them that the repetition of prayers of praise is good and so are prayers that spontaneously arise from deep within to fit the context of our lives.

The context of our lives, and especially the lives of grandchildren and our future progeny, are changing. I believe the change will be perilous. I believe that we parents, grandparents, spiritual educators and everyone who loves children need to do some radical thinking about how we teach the children to pray.

Let's start with the Johnny Appleseed grace. Googling this prayer reveals that there are multiple verses. I was thinking about asking our family to write a new verse that befits our times, so I was interested in all of those additional verses already out there in the world. However, I was disappointed by the quality of most of the verses I found online. They weren't written as prayers for a world where apple trees might disappear along with so many other species of plants and animals. I knew my family could do better, so we experimented with adding our own verse. The Johnny Appleseed grace, as sung by my family, still includes the first verse I shared with you above. Then, here is the new verse we now sing at family gatherings, such as Alison's 17th birthday:

I too can sow some seeds
And care for apple trees
So even many years from now
Children will know exactly how
The Lord cares for our needs.
Amen! Amen! Amen!

The table grace that has for generations been the staple of Whitt family meals is:

For food,
For friends,
For sunny days,
Dear Lord, we give you children's praise. Amen.

That is a lovely and memorable prayer that still calls to mind all the ways Grandma Whitt nurtured us. She was an extraordinary baker of apple pies and cinnamon rolls. Every time we visited, she hid a plate of sugar cookies somewhere in the house. However, what about a prayer that covers the not-so-sunny days? And praying for other children who need our care? Try this additional verse:

We thank you Lord for every day,
Even when the skies are gray.
We pray to learn to know and care,
For all the children everywhere. Amen.

Let's continue to keep this simple. Let's take a look at bedtime prayers. Meals and bedtimes are, of course, the most common times we teach children to pray. One such nighttime petition familiar to millions of us is:

Now I lay me down to sleep,
I pray the Lord my soul to keep.
Keep me safely through the night;
And, wake me with the morning light.

Let's add:

Bless my friends, the whole world bless;
Help me to learn helpfulness.
I know you keep me in your sight,
Even when things don't go right.

Could you and I, and thousands of others, take on the project of reshaping prayers for children? Could we share re-formed prayers in church newsletters, web pages, Sunday school curriculum and the practice of our families?

So, wherever I go, I urge adults: Teach the children to pray! Teach the children so that they learn they can count on God, in all circumstances. Teach them that they are unconditionally loved, no ifs ands or buts. Just Loved! Oh, and make a commitment to pray for each child God has put in our care, by name, every day and make it personal, specific and powerful. Pray like you mean it. Be prayer. Be Love.

For example, I will try to be prayer and love for Alison:

Maker of Heaven and Earth, Lord of Life, you are perfect love.

I thank you God that you are surrounding Alison with this love as her new day begins. You are riding beside her in her red 2006 Corolla as she drives to school, before the sun rises, for swim practice. You are keeping her strong in the presence of her peers. She is being herself, living her own values, no matter the pressures of others.

Knowing how much she is loved, she is facing a quiz in chemistry with confidence. In history class she is thinking her own thoughts about what is true and what is right. Help her remember how much the people who know her best respect her ability to take a stand and not back down.

Even when she is so busy that she forgets to ask for help, God you are helping her to carry the burdens that come her way. You are easing the trials that confront her among her friends and her family. You are strengthening her in self-discipline so she can pursue her goals with every expectation of success.

You, the God of her understanding, are never judging or condemning Alison. You are always on her side, never rejecting, always accepting. In this way you and others who love her are trusting her to correct her mistakes and learn from every failure. In your good and perfect time, help her to find the purpose of her life and to find the people who will help her to live that purpose in fullness and with grace.

Alison is finding hope and being love. Amen.

In crafting this prayer, I included Alison by name, visualized her and thought about her. Her deep sense of integrity, responsibility, intelligence and maturity has suggested to me for many years that God has a great purpose for her life. As I have said, I fully expect her to find that great purpose in the midst of a perilous global future.

So, I ask you: How do you prayerfully support the children you love as they find hope and become the love that the world desperately needs in a future of perils?

You and I love our children. We have chosen to acknowledge the likely truth that the future will be full of perils for our children. How do we live with this knowledge? How do we find peace of mind? For me, the indispensable answer lies partly in the loving work of praying my beloved children into the infinitely loving hands of God. Repeatedly, when I feel afraid for them—or guilty for my own role in this unsustainable culture of greed and planetary abuse—I surrender my children into God's keeping.

Finally, it is important to let your children know that you are praying for them, including the content of those prayers. When I gave my granddaughter Alison a devotional book recently, I taped my prayer for her inside the front cover.

Who knows what good such prayers might do? God knows. Someday, the children we love may also see the power and love behind our prayers and decide that they too can become this love.

Of course, there are other forms of prayer—some of them that I admit are beyond my own skill set. For example, I took yoga for seven years, but I have never taught it to children. I have read William Meyer's, *Three Breaths and Begin: A Guide to Meditation in the Classroom*, but have not implemented his instruction. I urge you to be adventurous as you explore how you will foster a family tradition of prayer. Our children need disciplines of prayer and meditation that will serve them for a lifetime. They need to have effective ways to maintain body-mind-spirit health. They need ways to release stress and transcend the perils they will face. I can also recommend Susan Verde's beautiful children's book, *I Am Yoga*. Read it for your own sake. Read it to your children. Begin your own practice. Pay special attention to everything Susan says at the end of the book in her "Author's Notes" to adults. By the time I finished studying those notes, I knew that I could easily get myself ready to begin a simple beginner's class with children. You can do this, too!

Friends, our children need to know how to do such things and they will need to be very practiced in these skills. They are fundamental to finding hope and being love.

Start now.

13

What Will Happen Next? It's Up to You

I said to my soul, be still, and
Wait without hope.
For hope would be hope for the wrong thing.
T.S. Eliot

Job discovered that being in God's presence is the source of our hope. What Eliot reminds us is that it's all too easy to place our hope in the wrong things.

Here are some expressions of hope that are *not* grounded in God's presence that I have heard during my interviews for this book:

- I hope to die before my family has to experience the consequences of climate chaos, resource depletion or economic collapse.
- I hope that my children will not be the ones who have to live with the worst consequences of societal collapse.
- I hope a president of my political party is elected before humanity's predicaments cause massive suffering in my country.
- I hope that the lobsters, shrimp, coho salmon and my other favorite seafoods don't disappear from the oceans before I get to dine at my favorite seafood restaurant a few more times.

- I hope that I can protect myself from—and can cope with—the grief and despair caused by all the bad things happening in the world.
- I hope they come up with the technologies we need soon, before they diminish my lifestyle.
- I hope my family will soon move away from the most dangerous locations, like at-risk coastlines.

False hope is experienced on the shaky-quaky ground of current circumstance. False hope surrenders to powerlessness. False hope takes no responsibility for the future. False hope is sinking in the quicksand of denial—hoping against all odds that things will work out, "as we hope."

Our circumstances cannot be trusted as the ground of hope. Every life is punctuated with disappointment. A child's pet dies. Best friends move away. Parents divorce. The soldier we love does not come home from war. A neighbor's child dies of leukemia. Storms decimate communities. Life and death are always partnered as one reality. No exceptions anywhere in the universe. Species, like the dinosaurs, arise and then pass from the Earth. No one dodges this reality. In the midst of an unimaginable variety of possible tragedies that cannot be prevented, our hope is in the fact that resurrection always transcends death. Termination begets creation. And amidst all of this, God is with us. That is our hope.

Let me share a series of quotes from interviews with parents, grandparents, friends, authors, scientists and spiritual leaders. These are common answers to the question: Knowing what you know about the predicaments humanity faces, what keeps your hope alive? These answers reflect the varied struggles of people anxious to find a ground for hope in perilous times.

The children.

My hope is in our children making a better world.

My hope is in the stories I hear of people who are changing the world.

My hope is in heaven. Jesus is coming soon.

I believe all the religions have to unite, and they will.

My hope was restored by the last elections.

My hope will be restored by the next election.

I know we will develop new sources of energy.

I know God will stop us from destroying ourselves.

Our only hope is population control.

Trusting God.

My children are smarter than me.

Young adults are going to fix the problems we could not.

Nuclear fusion.

Putting an end to war.

Bill Gates.

The blood of Jesus.

Humanity is resilient.

God will eventually fix everything.

Our children.

Faith—only faith.

The Earth will cure itself.

Keeping my focus on the good things, like the life choices of my sons.

Limiting attention paid to the bad things in the news.

Jesus.

Nature is correcting our mistakes.

Everything will turn out right. Just wait and see.

How do I answer this question?

My grandchildren give me hope. They brighten my days. When I heard my grandson Maxton promise God that he will become a scientist who rescues animals, I felt a burst of hope like the rising of the sun. I fully expect that given half a chance, Maxton will fulfill his promise, or some other equally significant promise. But I know that he and all the other promising children of his generation will not stop the ongoing extinction of thousands of species of animals and thousands more varieties of plants. Even more, I know that if fixing the devastating damage we have already done to the Earth community is the foundational source of Maxton's hope—he might well be disappointed and could succumb to despair. Given changing times and circumstances, Maxton, and all of us, must constantly reevaluate, imagine anew and work towards the next best possibility.

The need for loving action will never end. Love never fails. We experience hope every day when we seek to take the next right loving action, knowing that no matter the result, God is present.

Children already are aware of the perils we face. I have learned from Morgan, who I introduced in the last chapter, many details I had not known about how plastic straws, bags, bottles, toys, cups, food containers are a threat to marine life. In no uncertain terms she told me what she is doing about it, and what I should do about it. She had no trouble speaking her mind. My wife and I were persuaded and have launched our own campaign against plastics. We have found we have allies everywhere. For example, if we tell a waitress in a restaurant that we do not want plastic straws, we are likely to hear something like, "Oh, you are saving the turtles."

We say, "Yes." Smiles all around.

Hope smiles down on us as we collectively take these small actions. However, I am a realist. I have learned more about these threats to the oceans. I know that all the children in the world who are concerned about this crisis—plus all the adults who love them—are not enough to stop catastrophic production of more plastics before even more damage is done. What then?

Then, I will reimagine what love requires. And, I will act accordingly.

A Dance of Infinitely Loving Importance

Hope grounded in God's presence realizes that everything has a terminal destiny. We will die. Like peanut butter and jelly, life and death are partners. We are supposed to dance with our partners. So, dance, creatively, wildly, lovingly, while it is still the season of the dance. Live the way life is meant to be lived, aware that the time is short and thus precious beyond all imagination. Living rightly is a source of hope because doing the "next right thing" is always an achievable goal.

It is critical to realize that our Western industrial civilization has a terminal destiny. It will die, like every civilization before it. As a dance partner, I can reject my response-*ability* and let the civilization and all its life-denying idols—war, prejudice, fear, greed and on and on—lead the dance. Or I can take the lead and accept my capacity to change some of the steps. I cannot be the light penetrating all darkness, but I can light up the lives of those around me and I can dance as if my life counts for something of infinitely loving importance.

When I write and talk and teach like this, some people respond positively—and others ignore me and retreat into their denial. In those cases, I hear things like, "There is plenty of oil for the next hundred years." Or: "Climate change is a hoax." Or: "The technocrats already have the solutions. They will use them soon enough."

I have been accused of promoting despair. And, my first response is: What's wrong with despair? Despair is an altogether appropriate response to our collective actions that have killed billions of animals and destroyed vast stretches of habitat for humans and animals. Amidst the days of my life, it is entirely appropriate and inevitable that I will cycle in and out of despair. What I hope for the children I love is that they will have the resilience, emotional maturity and especially spiritual depth to pass through the pain of loss and, on the other side, find hope and be love all over again.

Maxton, Morgan and millions of others, children and adults, can all dance as if their lives are wondrous gifts of Just Love. This is a source of hope. Right living. Right loving.

Yes, I believe that we are living in the historical era of humanity's collective failure to live in harmony with God's creation. Resource depletion and climate chaos, though most of us barely notice them, are overtaking us far faster than individuals and collectives can respond. I cannot just wait, hang out and keep silent until I am certain about how soon and bad things are going to get. Some words must be spoken now, and some decisions must be acted upon, now. Deciding and acting—even if I am wrong about a particular next step I plan to take—are an expression of hope grounded in reality. Hope, grounded in the knowledge and experience of God as Just Love, will sometimes lose its focus and courage. Still, like in the parable of the Prodigal Son, hope knows the way home.

Love is counting on me. And, should I fail, even if I die, love continues. Even though everything I love might perish from the Earth, Love does not end. After all, nothing can separate us from the love of God, and nothing can stop the unfolding of the purposes of Love throughout the creation. God continues to say of creation: "It is very good." Stars are born and die, and species may disappear from the Earth, but God's Love is eternal. That spirit will not cease when I die. Neither will I.

The Seductive Power of False Hopes

Early this morning, I ate a breakfast of free-range chicken eggs, Amish-made bread and a gala apple from a local orchard. During breakfast, I continued watching the movie, *A Theory of Everything*. The film tells the story of professor Stephen Hawking, his scientific brilliance, devastating disease, universe-penetrating insights, loves and beliefs.

Near the end of the film, Hawking is on a speaking tour to the United States and is asked this question: "You have said you do not believe in God. Do you have a philosophy of life that helps you?"

The professor answers: "It is clear that we are just an advanced breed of primates on a minor planet orbiting around a very average star in the outer suburb of one among a hundred billion galaxies. But, ever since the dawn of civilization, people have craved for an understanding of the underlying order of the world. There ought to be something very special about the boundary conditions of the universe. And, what can be more special than that there is no boundary? And there should be no boundary to human endeavor. We are all different. However bad life may seem, there is always something you can do, and succeed at. While there is life, there is hope."

The audience erupts with a standing ovation. As I watched this scene, my skin erupted with goose pimples. Tears leaped from my eyes. My inner thoughts formed the words, "I love this guy. It's past time to read his book, *A Brief History of Time*. I need his brand of bravery and hope, no matter what!"

Then, as I went back over Hawking's words—I began to see holes. He refers to people, "since the dawn of civilization" craving understanding of the world's "underlying order." Here's the hole I see: While I agree that humans have an innate hunger to understand, what if all the knowledge we accumulate leads to self-destructive behaviors? The longing for knowledge, in itself, is not a basis for hope.

He goes on to describe our universe as having "no boundary." Here's the hole I see: What does a universe without boundaries have to do with hope? I have been present with many people during their dying. No one has ever said to me that they were thankful that the universe has no boundaries. I have never tried to counsel hope in the midst of tragedies by reminding the suffering that we live in a limitless universe. Infinite immensity, in and of itself, is not a basis for hope.

Hawking insists "there should be no boundary to human endeavor." Here, I just have to disagree. Who thinks that is a healthy value? Maybe the builders of the Tower of Babel. The majority of human beings on planet Earth are living in survival mode, trapped by cultural and economic boundaries. Truth be told, too many limits and too few limits are both destroying our planetary home and many of its inhabitants. No hope here.

Hawking: "We are all different." Well, that's an obvious truth. But it does not connect to underlying values about how we should accept those differences. I wish he had said a whole lot more about our responsibilities to each other. Without the capacity to transcend our differences, those four words in his talk simply name one of many forces that continue to threaten the human adventure on this planet.

Hawking said: "However bad life may seem, there is always something you can do, and succeed at." For myself, I am grateful beyond words that there are many things I may strive for, but there are no guarantees that I will succeed at any of them. The capacity to strive can be a source of hope. It is for me. But for millions of starving children, no opportunity to strive exists and no such hope exists. There has to be something more for humanity to hold onto than the ability of some of us to strive and thrive.

Hawking: "Where there is life, there is hope." With all due respect to Dr. Hawking, this kind of hope seems like a bad joke. A person living with cancer and suffering intolerable pain needs a more solid hope than just being alive. If nuclear war or climate catastrophe or global economic collapse causes global suffering on a cataclysmic scale, who among us would be able to find hope in the mere declaration, "Well, at least I am alive!"?

I am taking this time to describe this movie, and my responses, because this experience illustrates how easy it is to be lured by seemingly hopeful words—enhanced by Hollywood moviemaking. As I watched the movie for the first time, my own spirits soared with the cheering crowd in that climactic scene. It took me a while to appreciate the shallowness of this affirmation. If I can be so misled, what defense do the children have from the purveyors of glitzy toys and games that they absolutely must own in order to be happy?

Their main defenders are the adults who love them and manifest this love with walks in the woods, stories that inspire, songs to remember, relevant and memorable prayers, moments of wonderment under a glorious night sky, exposure to marvelous diversities like people and cultures, undistracted attention and appreciation.

The ball has been passed to you. What is the next way you will spend hope-filled and loving time with a child?

Finding the Gift in the Grief

Many readers of this book are familiar with the five stages of grief as they were outlined by Elizabeth Kubler-Ross: Denial, bargaining, anger, depression and acceptance. Adults experience these stages, many times, in their lives and families.

Like most adults, I am acquainted with grief. Just a few examples: As a child we moved away from friends, multiple times. As a youth I was cut from both the basketball and the baseball teams. In college, I was rejected by a fraternity. As a young pastor, my dream of being the beloved servant of all the people was crushed, more than once. The deaths of my brother John and his wife Janet, within a matter of months, made the denial of my own mortality impossible to maintain. At retirement, Kathy and I pursued a dream of building upon my dad's legacy on the family homestead we lovingly called, "Whitt's End." That dream simply ended and we moved on.

However, in every case, something providential was waiting for us at the end of each season of grief, no matter how profound the loss. What if—knowing that Just Love is always seeking the next best loving possibility for us—we can always live with hope? What if we truly embrace the truth that, in one form or another, new and abundant life is always on its way? An asteroid, thousands of years ago, blasted our planet, terminated the dinosaurs and left tiny mammals to repopulate the earth—to the delight of foxes, wolverines, kangaroos, dogs and you and me. Not a bad gift, from humanity's point of view.

What if we truly believe that death is always followed by resurrection? What if we live our lives trusting that nothing can separate us from God's Love?

Brilliant Souls Around Us

We always need hope. Yet, there are moments when our need is extreme. For me, one of those moments was my mid-1980s depression. There I was, like millions of other men and women who have experienced depression—lost in shadows.

Then, in various times of daily devotions, I began to sense that Jesus had a message for me. That message included the insight that this season of personal darkness was important for me, and for the whole world as well. Just as I needed to be healed, so the world needed healing. As I learned to own my shadow, I began to experience healing, body, mind and spirit, of much multi-generational dysfunction. And, I saw that such healing could also come to all of humanity, the Earth community, the whole of creation.

This was, of course, a gift of transcendent purpose that, if believed, could foster endurance and thus life itself.

Skip ahead several decades to September 2019. I am reaching toward the stars for a way to explain this message of hope. Once again, I have been learning that my transformation, my courage, my love is critically important to the well-being of everyone and everything. I have also been learning that hundreds, thousands, millions, maybe billions of others, have been hearing the same message, what I would call the Word of the Lord.

Are you hearing it? We are all in this together. The critical moment is today. The person is you. No time to wait. No time to waste. You can't ignore your role in this universal healing. Seek your healing, now. Seek love, right now! Transformation is upon us, has been upon us, and will soon be upon us. Each one has healed, is healing and can heal the whole. Everything is taking place within the eternal now.

There are a plethora of brilliant souls exploring this theme and announcing this healing and transformation of all. In the 20th century, Tielhard de Chardin got the ball rolling. Richard Rohr and Cynthia Bourgeault have been kicking it hard and fast, up and down the field. Today, on the field of my life and learning, Ilia Delio, author of *The Unbearable Wholeness of Being*, has possession of the ball. She is trying to pass the ball to me. As I can catch it, I am passing it to you.

If you catch the pass—and are confused about what is happening— take a long trip back in time and imagine what it was like when there was another leap forward in consciousness. Imagine the first creature becoming self-aware—and knowing she was self-aware—and trying to grasp what in the creation was going on. What an amazing journey the human ones have been having for many millennia on this planet.

And now it is time for another leap forward. The ball is yours!

This is our hope. Something is happening within the Whole that is beyond our comprehension and outside our control. We can and will solve some problems and alleviate some suffering and impact the future in some very positive ways. We also know that we cannot fix all the predicaments—damaged creation, depleted resources, systemic injustice, suffering of the innocent.

Nonetheless, God is present among us and within us. Love is running down the field and is about to pass the ball, to you. Be there.

It all depends on you. God is Just Love. Be this Love.

14

What Does Love Require?

Open my eyes that I may see
Glimpses of truth You have for me.
Place in my hands the wonderful key
That will unlock and set me free.
Silently now I wait for You,
Ready my God Your will to do.
Open my eyes, illumine me, Spirit divine!

Clara Scott

How do we prepare ourselves and our children for the coming perils? As we face the future, we find two choices: Do what fear dictates. Or, do what love requires. Let's take a look at each path.

Choice 1: Do What Fear Dictates

How closely do you follow daily headlines? I follow the daily news, but just what is sufficient to keep me informed about the overall happenings in our nation and in the world. Too little news, and I become disconnected from human activity. Too much news and I become disconnected from my faith in God's activity in the world.

Early each day, I check out the lead articles in *The New York Times* and *The Washington Post*. For a faithfully Christian perspective on events and issues, I read *Sojourners* magazine cover to cover—plus, their email updates. My reading plan related to this book included lots of other articles and books on current issues. For example, I have become very well informed about the racism behind mass incarceration—and the scapegoating that causes many Christians to see LGBTQIA communities as enemies.

Collectively, this reading convinces me that fear is the dominant force behind far too much of the decision-making that passes for governance in the United States and globally. Just Love rarely enters the daily storyline of our nation and our world. When it does, I read with great interest and gratitude for those who rule with justice and compassion.

Fear divides America. Fear determines, for example, our policy towards immigrants. This fear will become far more threatening as climate chaos turns the current river of refugees into a tsunami. Fear bypasses thoughtful, wise and loving decision-making. Fear ignores ethical discernment. Fear, a cause of denial, impedes us from taking seriously the forces, factors and failures that are rapidly propelling humanity towards collapse.

Choice 2: Do What Love Requires

What does love require?

When I am obeying the law, I don't ask a question like that. I just obey the law. Loving my neighbor, however, requires more careful discernment. The law tells me that I have to exchange certain information with the other driver if I am in an automobile accident. But do I treat that driver to a display of road rage or to an expression of kindness?

The Golden Rule, found in one version or the other in the teaching of all the great world religions, suggests the moral standard of relating to others the way I want them to relate to me. The two great commandments, according to Jesus, are to love God and neighbor. I am to love my neighbor as I love myself. Do you and I always know how to love ourselves? Are we taking good care of ourselves amidst the competing demands of our lives? If not, how can you possibly know how to love a neighbor? And what about loving the stranger and the enemy? Decisions like these require something far more difficult than obedience to a law. They require discernment. Such acumen requires that we first ask the question, "Here and now, what does love require?" That question requires, for me as a Christian, that I seek the wisdom of Scripture and God's guidance.

Trust in the LORD with all your heart,
and do not rely on your own insight.
In all your ways acknowledge him,
and he will make straight your paths.
Do not be wise in your own eyes;
fear the LORD, and turn away from evil.

Proverbs 3:5-7 (NRSV)

And that, my friends, is where we run into big trouble because seeking God's guidance requires that we have a relationship with God. And that relationship requires that we be on a spiritual journey. And even then, discernment is often very difficult. For all of us, that difficulty requires that we have a community that encourages us and critiques our decision making. All of this is the foundation for answering that question: What does love require?

Remember, we are on a journey. Like Father Abraham and Mother Sarah, we don't know where we are going, and we don't know how to get there. Also, like Abraham, we will make consequential mistakes and will need to be forgiven and to make corrections. You and are I stepping out right now—me as I type and you as you read. We are about to come to a moment of decision. Let's imagine this point of decision as a traffic circle. What will you do? How will you become what your children need you to be? Where will you exit the traffic circle? In what direction will you proceed?

I suggest that prior to every decision, you give thanks. Tell God something like: "My God, thank you God that I only have to navigate one traffic circle at a time. Remind me, each and every day, hour and minute, that I only need to know what love requires of me one decision at a time. I don't need to worry about the future. I only need to live in the present."

If hymns work for you, find a hymnal and sing out loud:

Guide Me O Thy Great Jehovah, pilgrim through this barren land.
I am weak, but Thou are mighty—Hold me with Thy powerful hand …

Let the fire and cloudy pillar lead me all my journey through ...
When I reach the river Jordan, bid my anxious fears subside.

We're singing for our lives here. We are choosing between fear and love. Fear wants us to attack the messenger, to see our neighbor as our enemy. The more we learn, the pressure mounts. The weather is becoming more and more chaotic. Resources, particularly cheap energy, are being depleted. Thousands of species are becoming extinct. Fires are burning. Topsoil is disappearing and drinkable water is becoming scarce. Proposed solutions, such as more nuclear power plants, come with consequences that are extremely difficult to evaluate. The planet can't indefinitely support 7.7 billion people. Governments are becoming more autocratic.

Eventually, we realize that our independent lifestyles are too costly. They are not sustainable. We must begin to teach, by example, the skills and attitudes and values associated with living sustainable lives.

Finding Hope and Being Love Within Community

I am a Christian whose beliefs and values are grounded in Scripture. I strive, above all, to be Christ-like, to be "in Christ" at all times and in all things. What does being "in Christ" have to do with my consumer lifestyle? For Jesus, the most frequently addressed moral and spiritual issue is our relationship with money. Whether you are a Christian or not, there is great benefit in traveling back in time with me to encounter the lives of the earliest followers of Jesus, as we meet them in the Bible's book of Acts.

Jesus was murdered by the principalities and powers of the world: political, economic and religious powers. After Jesus's death, his followers at first were terrified, fearing that his fate would be theirs. They were right, though not in the way they envisioned it. Jesus defeated death—and so did they. They became powerful, so powerful that fear was diminished. They stopped being so afraid of their oppressors. They stopped being so afraid of poverty. They even were conquering their fear of death.

What happened next? Here is the story from Luke, who wrote both the Gospel of Luke and the book of Acts:

All who believed were together and had all things in common; they would sell their possessions and goods and distribute the proceeds to all, as any had need. Day by day, as they spent much time together in the temple, they broke bread at home and ate their food with glad and generous hearts, praising God and having the goodwill of all the people.

Acts 2:44-47 (NRSV)

That's the story. That's the testimony of Luke. At the very least we ought to honor the witness of the early church by being accountable to other believers for how we use our money. We are talking here about the lifestyle of the earliest Christians, those who breathed the same air as Jesus. Today, few Christians care to talk much about this kind of passage. Hardly any are open to even discuss what it would be like to live out our faith in community, less encumbered by riches.

The critical question this book raises is: How do we prepare our children to find hope and to be love in a future of perils? The answer I have explored through these chapters is: in communities, where Just Love is known and lived. In community—knowing that God is Just Love, knowing that all are one, knowing that my neighbor is myself—we can literally live more with less. All kinds of community arrangements can free up resources to help others in need—and there are going to be a lot more needy people in the years to come. In community we can destroy much less and preserve much more, giving our children and grandchildren and all the greats to come a better chance at making a good life for themselves and others.

Consider some options.

When I think about the children I love, and their parents, actual communes have never been on my mind—but my children have taught me a lot about the possibilities of community. Back in 2007, before they had children of their own, my daughter Lauren and her husband, Jeff, went on a mission trip to build homes for families in El Salvador through the Fuller Center for Housing. On their way back home, Lauren found herself unable to abide even the thought of living in their spacious suburban home alone. She and Jeff began praying and pondering and eventually decided to invite friends from their church, who were struggling to pay both living and education expenses, to move in with them. These friends, and others from their church, have continued to be part of a small support group that is now in its second decade. Small groups and house churches are both viable options for those seeking stronger bonds to communities. Today, Lauren and Jeff share their home with foster children. The challenges of that commitment to children would be impossible without the communities that support them.

I learned recently about a community of young Christians in Cincinnati who have founded the Madison Place community, mplacec.org online. By sharing a common purse, they are able to dedicate extraordinary resources to drug recovery programs and other services for the urban poor.

My wife and I spent a week at a Bruderhof community, following traditions established a century ago in Europe. I believe you will be deeply impressed, if you decide to discover for yourself what Christian community means at the Bruderhof, bruderhof.com online. Our visit was exhausting, revealing and life changing. We learned that these Christians struggle, as we do, with materialistic longings and must consciously and conscientiously strive to live by the values of the New Testament church. We will visit again. These brothers and sisters are now part of our community, the one that keeps us honest before God.

I recently began an affiliation with a 40-year-old Christian community in rural Massachusetts called Agape, agapecommunity.org. They have been a faithful witness for peace and justice for many years and now are seeking to discover anew what it means to be community in this fateful era of human history.

In 2019, Kathy and I moved to the community of Hide-A-Way Hills, Ohio. There are over 700 homes in our neighborhood, all nestled in the hills near Hocking Hills State Park. We are pondering and praying about ways we can strengthen the experience of community, neighbors helping neighbors, serving others, wisely using resources, within an established neighborhood association where there is already a great deal of mutual support.

On various websites that talk about sustainable living, I have read stories about extended families where all the scattered family units have chosen to come back together in an area where, as things change in our country, they will be better able to support each other, whenever the need arises. Other families with the resources to invest and the courage to begin, are trying to get ahead of the learning curve by beginning now to learn the skills needed by a new breed of American pioneers. They are buying farms, learning how to raise livestock, grow and store food, weave their own cloth, survive and lead good lives, even if Western industrial society collapses.

Native Americans, and other indigenous peoples, are relearning and practicing their old ways, including knowledge of healing and sustainable agriculture. There are many First Nation people in the United States who are committed to living once again in harmony with the lands and animals around them. European industrial ways of abusing the Earth will perish from the Earth, they are certain. They will work to heal the wounds the invaders have left behind.

What does love require of you and me? What forms of community could Just Love lead us to discover? For Christians, a group could gather to read and discuss the remarkable book, *Called to Community: The Life Jesus Wants for His People*, which includes articles by Dietrich Bonhoeffer, Joan Chittister, Mother Teresa, Richard Foster, Dorothy Day and many others.

Our Gifts to the Future

We live in a materialistic culture where money is god and consuming is worship. The evangelists of this religion are the most persuasive and best-paid purveyors of their religion to be found anywhere in the world. Their purpose is to sell, not only products, but also a vision of the good life. We have bought into this vision at the cost of our souls, and now, it seems, at the cost of our very survival on planet earth. And yet, for the most part, we consume on and on and on.

Spiritual development is the most important task of the communities we must create in order to change course and to prepare our children to find hope and be love in the future. Few adults are going to change course unless they do so in community. Few children will be prepared adequately for their future outside of community. We have to do this spiritual work together.

Together, adults and children in community will share experiences, sing songs, tell stories and come to know God as Just Love. We will learn that we are one, that we are connected to everything and everyone. It has never been more important for all of us to know our proper relationship to all creatures great and small, and everything else. Our children must know the story of their place in the universe, their role in the unfolding purpose of God.

Our children will be our messengers to the future. Doesn't that give you a sense of your ultimate purpose on this earth, right now, even in the midst of perils?

Life Decisions, Vocations, and Skills

Amidst all the things we cannot control in this era of human history— there are a host of actions we can take. Here's an example:

In the 1970s, Bob and Sharon made sure each of their seven children got to attend the college of their choice. Each chose a liberal arts education and then went to graduate school within the professions of teaching, engineering, medicine and computer science. Good choices were made. All found fulfilling jobs and earned good livings. Today? They are thinking a lot about the educational choices their grandchildren will make. They would like to be sure the grandchildren know that they are living in a transitional era of human history. They would like to tell them that the money and time you invest in education may or may not serve you in the future. The world order is changing, fast. Some skills, like engineering skyscrapers, could become irrelevant. They are thinking of asking their children and grandchildren to talk about investing educational resources differently—including in skills their children are learning that might be valuable in a collapsing economy. They want to make sure the children are learning sustainability skills like cooking on an open fire, organic gardening, animal husbandry, woodworking with hand tools and spiritual and emotional care. The demand for these services will exceed the supply someday soon, they think.

Decision-making in this family is being guided by their awareness of changing circumstances. Our world is changing. Everybody's circumstances are changing. We can adapt. More needs to be said about the decisions we will be making. Please return with me to the traffic circles metaphor.

Our children and grandchildren will never enter the traffic circle that Kathy and I are driving around right now. We will never enter many of the circles they are encountering. It is staggering to step back and realize what a difficult decision we are facing at this very moment. The confusion we feel as we enter our next circle of choices ought to give us pause when we begin considering advising anyone else, especially our children, on where they should exit. However, sometimes silence is not golden. Silence can be cowardly and dangerous. To speak or not to speak? Answers require wise discernment.

When we moved to our retirement home in the beautiful hills and woods of southeastern Ohio, in 2019, neither of us was possessed by the certainty that industrial civilization had begun crashing. We only saw in part. Still, I began preaching sermons on the environmental crisis in the mid-1970s. Both Kathy and I acknowledged years ago some of coming perils, including the instability of the global economy, built, as it is, upon unsustainable debt, staggering gaps between the rich and the poor and unkeepable promises. We have been grieving for many years humanity's failure to steward the creation, including the extinction of thousands of species of animals and plants. Since the previous century, we have known that there are limits to growth. Earth cannot indefinitely support 7.7 billion people.

We have been recycling for many years and steadily making choices to decrease our carbon footprint. However, only in 2019, as I did reading and research for this book, was I convinced of the immediacy and severity of our global predicaments. Kathy was doing her own research and was uncovering additional information and insights.

We are facing some hard truths:

- Collapse of the systems that sustain human life on this planet has begun. Collapse will continue. We face a morass of intersecting predicaments.
- Denial will continue and time needed for positive adaptation will continue to be wasted, especially by the principalities and powers of the world, including governments, corporations and other large institutions like religious denominations.

- These truths are being accepted by some and positive deep adaptations have already begun among individuals and communities possessed by courage and love.
- Much damage to the ecosystem cannot be repaired. There is no going back to any "good old days."
- Our children, grandchildren and great-grandchildren will experience a world that bears little resemblance to one they were born into.
- In that world there will be unparalleled suffering. The suffering will be scattered and enormously unfair. The poor will be its earliest and severest victims.
- In this universe, death is always followed by resurrection.

Let that sink in.

The fact that in this universe, death is always followed by resurrection, was not a conclusion Kathy and I have quickly or easily applied to today's circumstances. Our belief in this fact, and our capacity to ground our hope on this fact, comes and goes. Still, decisions have to be made. At a previous family decision circle, months ago, we decided to seek to know the truth about the predicaments that threaten all life on this planet. Just Love required this of us and has given us the strength and wisdom needed to follow through. We have not wavered from that choice, and God has proven entirely able to care for us. In our stumbling and fumbling way, we are sharing this decision with others. We get through the emotionally broken days and move on.

We also decided not to stop at simply knowing the truth—but also to live this truth we are coming to know. You've heard such encouragement before: "Vote with your feet." "Put your money where your mouth is." "Lead by example." Often it is difficult to decide what such advice means. We've driven around this traffic circle quite a few times, feeling confused and unable to "read the signs of the times." We have found that, ultimately, spiritual discernment is the only reasonable way to choose where we should go.

In our discernment process, Kathy and I became even more certain that we needed to continue implementing many previous decisions, like owning only one car, no international tourist travel by air, maintaining our organic and hydroponic gardens, supporting local farmers, recycling, composting and avoiding plastics. It was also helpful to keep remembering how strongly we felt God's guidance in moving to this specific home in Hide-A-Way Hills. It has helped that we have had a few months to notice how difficult it is for people in our lives to hear what we have to say about the current predicaments of humanity. Finally, after driving in circles for quite a while, we knew that we were being called to live well in two worlds at the same time.

Living Well in Two Worlds at the Same Time

Kathy and I have taken the exit toward—and have begun living in—two worlds at the same time. What does that mean?

Many years ago, Gandhi taught us: We are trying to live more simply so that others may simply live. We know that we can live well in the world around us, right now. At the same time, we can learn skills, practice sustainable development and join with others in community so that we are equipped to live in the world that could emerge depending on what catastrophes may circle the globe in coming years.

I describe this hopeful vision of preparation as living well in two worlds:

World 1—the present world where we have been planted—the one we have been building together for many years. We will remember that our abundance, skills, passions, resources, family and friends are all gifts of God. We choose not to abandon this world and its problems. We will keep doing justice, loving kindness and walking humbly with God. We will keep building communities that support major changes towards living sustainable lives.

World 2—in the future, we could be living in a more primitive world that may be a stage of collapse our children and grandchildren will be forced to live within. My primary goal is to teach the children I love that they can find ways to adapt no matter what happens around them. We are giving them examples right now. There's great family fun in learning how to build a campfire. We have learned how to bake our own bread, that we regularly share with our neighbors. This is a whole attitude toward family and community life that we can pass on to the next generations. Actions speak louder than words. Children learn far more from what we do than what we say. Our actions will make it more likely that they can survive, and even thrive. We will model for others that there are ways to positively adapt to changing circumstances—even though those circumstances may not be what we anticipate.

Given where Kathy and I live, the following are some adaptations we may make: We have a well. We can install a muscle powered water pump. We can build a woodburning cooking stove and a brick oven and learn how to use them. Build a root cellar and fill it up. Grow as much of our own food as reasonably possible. Preserve foods by canning. Install and use a composting toilet. Gather together the tools needed to cut firewood by hand. Weave cloth. Set aside a few "forever foods," like salt, instant coffee and sugar. Make topsoil. Reimagine, recreate, rebuild our home so that it could be habitable by more people—God only knows who. Those are enough ideas to get us started, and far more than we can afford now. But check us out this summer. Something will be different in our world.

So, what about your world? I am painfully aware that most of my readers likely do not live in the countryside. You are, right now as you read this, traveling on a different traffic circle than ours giving you a different set of options. I long for you to know that you have the ability to ask God for guidance, to discern what love requires, to make the next best choice.

However, I also know that it is possible you feel stuck in the circumstances of your life and our rapidly changing world—as if your car has broken down on the side of the road on a dark and frightening night. You and I may be at such different places in our lives that you are experiencing more fear and isolation than I am. If I could, I would offer a hug, a listening ear or some other expression of compassion. Maybe I could help you change that flat tire. Kindness is too often underrated.

What I can do is let you know: I am waiting to hear from you, to build community with you, to travel together with you. How joyful it would be if our journeys converge long enough that I can help you to celebrate your discovery of your path. Please, reach out.

What Must I Grieve Tomorrow?

Along the way, as I have emphasized throughout this book, we will encounter grief. I recently sat vigil for 14 hours at the bedside of a dear friend of more than 30 years. She was 95 and ready to die, but often dying does not come easy. When we were younger, Jean and I fought and lost some battles together over our mutual determination to focus our church's priorities on missions. When one of the worst things that could happen to a family happened to mine, Jean was at my home every school morning for six months to help me get the children ready for a new day. Such love one never forgets.

In my hours with Jean in her intensive-care room, we danced with every imaginable emotion. We wept and laughed and rested and got angry. We held on and let go. One thing we did not do was hold anything back. What needed to be said got said. Words of gratitude, affirmations of faith, remembrances of common losses and failures. Regrets. Celebrations. Up against the impending and inescapable approach of death, we lived and loved well. Love does not walk away from such painful stretches of time. They are embraced.

Death is embraced—if we can learn how to overcome the fear of death. In my 70 years as a person and a pastor, I have embraced this inevitable and fearsome passage many times. Love has seen me through. Whether you are conscious of it or not, you and I have been preparing for everything that is coming next for our entire lives. We were given this time, and no other. This life, and no other. These little ones to love.

You and I are strange creatures. We can love and grieve at the same time. We can laugh and cry at the same time. Whenever we are living and loving alongside anyone who is suffering, we are learning how to live and love well, no matter what loss is threatening to break us. Women have told me that that is the way it is with childbirth. The moment the baby appears, unbounded love supplants unparalleled pain and fear. For most women, I have been told, the love is so boundless that before too long they are more than willing to go through it all over again. Maybe that is something like what God experiences when the grief of infinite loss is experienced in tandem with the joy of infinite love.

Grief and love are both infinite, but love is so much bigger. Love never fails. Love never gives up. Love is never wasted. Love stares perils in the face and then, after a season of fear, re-enters a season of love. In a universe filled with Just Love, there is always something bigger than our losses, even though we cannot yet see it.

Love lets go of fear. Love teaches us—often not too easily or too quickly—not to fear grief and despair. In fact, if my own experience proves the point, it is on the road that passes through fear, grief, and despair that we learn that God is Just Love, that Love is inside us, and that we are never powerless to act on behalf of love.

Ready or not, let's get going.

What Can I Love Today?

I draw great strength and joy, each day, simply from remembering and listing all my moments, insights and experiences with love—little things, big things. Try it.

As an example, here's one of my daily lists:

- I loved cooking today: macaroni and cheese and blueberry muffins.
- I loved delivering some of each to our neighbors.
- I love envisioning a day when I can cook these in an outdoor, wood-fired oven.
- I loved working on this book and feeling both the grief and the inspiration that come and go as I am pondering and typing.
- I loved listening to Kathy's newest idea on how we can live abundantly and simply at the same time. She showed me how our basement could accommodate a root cellar.
- I loved reading a new children's book that came in the mail today, *When God Made You*, by Matthew Paul Turner. I love the book's wild colors and the characters in flight, and the message, "Over *you* God was smiling and already dreaming." I love the colorful, exuberant, childlike reminder that God made us all.

- I loved walking out the back door onto the deck in my slippers. The squirrels scattered as I slid open the door. The deer looked up from their cracked-corn chomping.
- I loved the hour of spiritual direction via Skype with a woman in New York. I loved listening to her image of God shifting, toward Just Love.
- I love life. I have long ago made my peace with the fact that life and love flow endlessly through an unpredictable sequence of despair and hope, sickness and health, sorrow and joy, disturbance and calm, unpleasantness and pleasure, guilt and forgiveness, fear leading to anger and trust leading to love.
- I love that, in the midst of darkness, I keep finding light.

I am learning to make peace with the extremities of the feelings that are inevitable as we confront the present problems and coming calamities. I am asked questions like this: How can you bear to contemplate a future so threatening? Why don't you give up?

I answer, in my most grace-filled moments, "Love bears all things." In fact, as my own experience shows, it is on the road that passes through fear, grief and despair that we learn that God is Just Love—and that Love is inside us—and that we are never powerless to act on behalf of Love.

Let's get at it.

I invite you once again to be the community forming among readers of this book. I'll be waiting to hear from you. My call is to join me—and countless other families—seeking hope and Just Love. There is great wisdom in our Scriptures about our quest.

> *Love is patient;*
> *love is kind;*
> *love is not envious or boastful or arrogant or rude.*
> *It does not insist on its own way;*
> *it is not irritable or resentful;*
> *it does not rejoice in wrongdoing,*

but rejoices in the truth.
It bears all things,
believes all things,
hopes all things,
endures all things.
Love never ends.

1 Corinthians 13 (NRSV)

100 Things Families Can Do To Find Hope and Be Love

Start with this list of 100 ideas and, before you know it, you won't need my list. You'll be making your own! Keep paper handy wherever you go so you can jot down your ideas. I have had this mindset for so long that ideas pop up throughout each day.

Just as I was finishing this list one morning, my wife Kathy was leaving on some errands. I handed her a short addition to the grocery list that included four boxes of salt.

"I probably need to explain why I want four boxes of salt," I said.

"I certainly would have wondered," she said.

"It's something we should do. I was just reading about foods that last forever—and one of them is salt. Remember those glass spaghetti jars we have saved? I am going to fill two of them with salt, then put those jars in our just-in-case shelves in the basement."

Kathy hugged me. "This is a weird day. This morning, God and I were just talking about sadness and grief in this mad world. God told me to give the birds a bit more food today. That's what I can do this morning."

"I get it!" I said, still hugging her.

And, in an instant, we had two more ideas—and we were acting on them.

You'll soon get your own ideas! To get you started, here are 100 ideas. *(And, if you don't like a few of them, don't be discouraged. I'll share a little secret: There are actually more than 100 here to ensure you have an abundance of challenges you'll enjoy!)*

- Remember that God's Just Love surrounds you. You live and move and have being in God's love. Simply start by reflecting on that truth for a second or a minute.
- Start a spiritual journey. And here's an encouraging tip: You've already started one by reading this book and, now, this list.
- Begin a daily devotional practice. If this is a new idea, there are many traditional resources from centuries-old cycles of daily prayer to very contemporary approaches to spiritual practices. You'll find some helpful books suggested in the final pages of this book.
- Learn more about the spiritual traditions of your family and your community. You may discover a tradition that will delight and inspire you.
- Make a habit of voicing small blessings and prayers throughout each day, like prayers after washing your hands or before a meal. There are many traditional prayers you could learn—or you could make up your own.
- Get lots of rest.
- Go for a long walk in the woods.
- Deep in the wilderness, sit and wait on the Lord.
- At night, find a dark place away from the lights of town and look up into the stars.
- Spend the night under the stars with your children.
- Move closer to your extended family—physically, emotionally, spiritually.
- Increase the time you spend with children you love.
- Show children a deeper relationship with the creation.
- Invite children to cook with you, especially family favorites that may include pasta, bread, stews and other hearty foods that are easy to make at home.
- Teach children to build a fire and cook on it.
- Teach children fun gardening projects, such as raising herbs in a pot or potatoes in a garbage can.

- Make French fries over a campfire with the potatoes you grew in a garbage can. Season them with your herbs.
- Read the children's book, *I Am Yoga*, with children, then use the instructions at the end of the book to begin practicing meditation with your children.
- Take children to a planetarium.
- Learn a new craft like spinning and weaving.
- Teach children hands-on arts-and-crafts traditions. Show them how to knit, crochet, weave or make pottery.
- Invite children into your workshop to learn woodworking.
- Make and set up a bird feeder with children.
- Dream up heroic roles children can play as celebrators and protectors of the creation.
- Invite your children to make up and act out a play—just for fun with family. Got old clothes stored in the house? Let them put on these "costumes" as they dream up a story.
- Pay attention as you talk with others—focusing more on listening than on what you plan to say in response.
- Pay attention as you read. That may be harder than you think. Try making notes as you read, perhaps even writing in the margins of a book. Have you written in the pages of this book already? Perhaps it's time to go back and re-read a favorite section.
- Decrease your family's debt, thus increasing your options and flexibility.
- Look closely at how your neighborhood functions. Make a list of all the systems that maintain life where you live. Start with water, electricity, transportation, the distribution of food, the disposal of waste. Envision all the living, breathing, moving systems in your neighborhood—and choose one that you can improve. Choose a first step in that improvement.
- How many of your neighbors rarely have human contact? Is there someone you could regularly visit—or occasionally call—to brighten their day or help with chores?

- Give away your second car to a person in need.
- Read a book on edible and medicinal plants. Look for these plants growing wild around you. Plant some of them in your garden.
- Be kind.
- Ponder the miracle of life. Give thanks for this miracle.
- Buy milk in returnable bottles.
- Learn about local farmers and food suppliers. Support local, sustainable farming.
- Visit a farm with children. Learn about animals, crops and the sources of our food.
- Watch a movie with teenagers about race in America. Talk about it with them.
- Learn what it means to become an anti-racist.
- Organize a "God Is Just Love" retreat.
- Look for wild berries together as a family.
- Learn about mushrooms and look for them in the right places and seasons.
- Take children fishing—or simply invite them to get wet and muddy and explore small streams and creeks.
- Build a collection of children's books that share the affirmations in this book. You'll find suggestions in the final pages of this book.
- Take part in a hands-on mission trip. Build something together.
- Visit and learn from people who are living simply.
- Recycle more.
- Put your children in charge of an important household goal—like recycling. You'll be surprised at how much more you recycle.
- Subscribe to a magazine that your whole family will want to read as you learn about the world. Then, actually read it together. Talk about it. Hang up pictures from it as reminders.

- Subscribe to a magazine that will help the adults in your household to understand global issues from a faith perspective, like *Sojourners*.
- Choose a spiritual director.
- Build a spiritual friendship.
- Balance the time you spend following the most important daily news events around the world—so that you don't wind up dwelling excessively on those news reports.
- Make a goal of spending as much time in prayer and spiritual practices as you do in following the news.
- Invite friends to let you know about concerns you can add to your daily prayer time.
- Jot down a prayer list. Keep it handy or carry it with you.
- If friends ask you what they can pray for, be prepared to tell them honestly about your concerns.
- As you rebalance your spiritual practices, make notes in a daily journal about how this balance is changing in your life.
- Learn to live hopefully in each moment you spend alone—and in the time you spend with friends, co-workers and loved ones. What gives you hope? What takes hope away?
- Consider sharing your home with another family. What would be involved if someone moved into your home with you?
- Physically visit family more than in the past.
- Virtually visit family even more often.
- Spend a day away from electronic gadgets—or a week.
- Give this book to someone else who loves children.
- Establish a book-reading group. Start with this book. Enjoy other books recommended in these pages.
- Plant a tree.
- Plant lots of trees.
- Make a list of all the parks within walking or biking distance of your home—and enjoy them one by one, inviting children to draw or make pictures of each one afterward.

- Make a list of all the parks within an hour's drive—and visit each one, enjoy and make pictures to hang on your walls.
- Plan to visit a different national park each year. Visit. Enjoy. Fill your life with stories and images from your outdoor adventures.
- Teach children some of your favorite songs, especially favorites from when you were young.
- Ask children to teach you their favorite songs. Learn them with as much enthusiasm as you teach your own songs.
- Visit a library together.
- Choose books you will read together and talk about as a family. Remember to let children choose some of the books!
- Build a project with hand tools—no electricity allowed.
- Attend a worship service with someone from another faith tradition.
- Invite friends from another tradition to visit during one of your family's favorite annual festivals—then visit them during one of their favorite holidays.
- Ask friends, neighbors and co-workers how to properly greet them during their holidays and festivals. Ask children about this, too, and they may surprise you by already knowing more than you do.
- Share your food with family, friends and neighbors. Planting a garden? Don't let your extra tomatoes go to waste. Learning to make bread? Don't let those extra loaves go stale and moldy.
- Learn about preserving foods from your garden. Beyond traditional canning, there is freezing, drying and other techniques that are fun and tasty.
- Just before the autumn frost, learn to make the most of crops left in the field. Wrap green tomatoes in old newspaper and store in a cool, dry place. Check back later and you will be surprised.
- Read more about resiliency and humility. Many new books are addressing these essential themes each year.
- Spend a week focusing on doing "the next right thing."

- Spend a week committed to seeing God in each new person you encounter. Read about what Dorothy Day and saints learned from this spiritual—and very practical—way of life.
- Set a goal of reading from the Bible each day. There are many plans online, some of which are quite easy to follow—and some of which are more ambitious, like reading the entire Bible in a year.
- If you normally read the Bible silently, try reading it aloud. Try reading it aloud repeatedly. Try reading it aloud with different inflections—and from different English translations.
- Learn about Native American spirituality.
- Spend more time in silence.
- Practice gratitude. Spend a day—or a week—focused on the many gifts we receive each day that are vital to our well-being. Try to keep up with expressing some form of gratitude for each one. It's a big challenge!
- Keep a gratitude journal. If you discover you can't keep up with acknowledging all the gifts you receive each day—at least commit yourself to writing about one gift each day in your gratitude journal.
- Weeks or months later, go back and read earlier entries in that journal either alone or with people you love. You may be surprised at what they add to your memories of these blessings.
- Write a prayer for each person you love, starting with each child in your life.
- Try writing a prayer for each person who you don't like! Want an even bigger challenge? Start by writing a prayer for a person you downright hate.
- Bring out interactive games and activities in your home that provide any-time connections like a jigsaw puzzle on a table in a family room. It's easy to take a few minutes out, here and there throughout a day, to gather with others and talk as you click the pieces into place.
- Set up a hummingbird feeder. Before you fill it, learn about the formulations hummingbirds enjoy. Make it a family rule to stop

everything and watch these delightful birds, if they suddenly appear.

- Discuss setting up a just-in-case storage area in your house. Discuss what items you will stock and who will be responsible for checking and rotating the basic inventory. If your system seems fun and flexible, you may find that children will eagerly play a role.

- Start simple with your just-in-case goal. Put together an emergency kit for your car. Then, organize an emergency shelf in your home for items you might need in a pinch. Start with simple items. Do you have to run to the store each time a light bulb blows or a nail or glue is needed for a simple fix?

- Learn about forever foods and, as you learn about each one, store some of it.

- Talk with your family about the items on this list of 100-plus ideas. Decide together what you will try next. And, invite family members to jot down more items that should be added to your shared list. Feel free to write in the margins of this book—but, if you take this seriously, you'll almost certainly need more paper very soon.

- Talk with your family about age-appropriate activities, so everyone is able to play a role in a project.

- Talk with your family about age-appropriate sharing, so you can share news, stories, songs and games that everyone will enjoy.

- Practice listening and discussing with others—and receiving critical feedback without defensiveness.

- Actually listen to what is said when you ask others, "How are you?"

- Remember what each person says and check back later in helpful ways. Tend to forget these things? Don't be shy about making a list or posting a reminder.

- Establish a few simple, weekly traditions that connect family, friends and neighbors like making sure to visit or phone someone once a week. When you do, spend as much time listening as talking.

- Consciously build diverse communities where you live, work and worship. Spend a week silently assessing how often you limit yourself to a single age group, or a single gender, or a single racial or ethnic group. You may be surprised at how limited your world has become. Change that.
- Sing more—alone and with others.
- Laugh more—alone and with others.
- In all things—be Just Love.

Acknowledgments

Christians speak of a great cloud of witnesses, some with us on this earth and others watching over us from eternity, who are a real presence lifting us out of the darkness into the light. I have so many of them to thank. I remember you. Mom and Dad, I love you.

Early readers, notably Dan Buttry, Kate Jacobs, David Miller and Sister Marise May cheered me on. Yet, during the Christmas season of 2018, a year into my research and writing project, I came to the self-awareness that I did not know how to complete this book. One of my readers, Dee Dee Turlington, then the president of the American Baptist Minister's Council and a good friend, told me point blank that I really needed an editor. In February of 2019, I found an editor and publisher. He immediately told me that I needed to rethink my opening chapter. There began much learning and a remarkable transformation of the message and its presentation. David Crumm, and his team at Read the Spirit Books, strangely believed in me even before I myself fully understood the potential of this book.

For the message of this book, I stand on the shoulders of giants and geniuses, the Godly, and the grace filled. I have so many of you to thank. I am grateful. St. Francis, Teilhard, Morton, Matthew, Walter, I remember you.

The production of the book and the angels and allies whose partnership sends forth the message into the world. I have so many of you to thank—and still counting.

I remember you and I promise that, by the mercy of God and the love of friends and family and the faithful, I will continue to shine forth the light that you have reflected into my life. With you I will celebrate the light, be the light. With you, I will find hope. With you, I will be love. Together we are learning how to help our children to find hope and to be love.

Throughout the past two and a half years, my wife Kathy has often functioned as a research assistant; that is when she was not functioning as a copy editor and a believer in me and the message. I often remind her how few women would, or could, travel side by side with someone writing a book like this one.

My brother Jim and his wife Jessie have also functioned in multiple roles, especially as explorers and disputers. Jim, as you are writing your book, I will gladly volunteer to be your grand disputer, or is that grand inquisitor?

I was truly like Abraham and Sarah, of Genesis fame, as I began my research and writing project on spirituality and science in January of 2018. I knew I was traveling somewhere important but had no idea where I would land. Then, I kept running into amazing teachers and guides. These encounters felt to me like an unending series of miracles. They were just there, when needed. I have so many of you to thank. Sr. Lois Barton. Dr. Peter Saulson. Dr. J. Scott Turner. The Rev. Michael Dowd. Dean Walker. Tim Hochstetler. Lee Doll. Some, like Joanna Macy, appeared to me in books and podcasts, others, like Brian McLaren and Michael Dowd, both in books and up close and personal. However, I doubt I ever would have recognized the call to write this book, or found the spirituality to undergird it, if I had not crossed paths, both in books and in person, with Fr. Richard Rohr, the Rev. Cynthia Bourgeault and William Paul Young at the Trinity Conference in 2016—and John Dominic Crossan at the Universal Christ conference in 2018.

Since moving to Hide-A-Way Hills, Ohio, in the natural wonderland known generally as Hocking Hills, we have made many treasured friends. Beloved among them is a 10-year-old girl named Morgan. She is so wise about, and so in love with, the things of creation.

During the Christmas season in 2019 I felt strongly the Spirit's tug to deepen my relationship with Sanctuary Church Columbus, a multi-ethnic congregation whose pastor, Rich Johnson, leads us as preacher, prophet and mystic. It is within these communities, and others, that the purpose of my life is unfolding and passing from vision to reality. Rich has also, with my deep appreciation, become very interested in this book.

My capacity to follow the calling to write this book has been absolutely dependent of the support and counsel of my latest three spiritual directors: Larry Reichley, Mark Lawson and Annie Dalby. All have taught me that the Spirit is the real director of all of our lives.

Even as I end these acknowledgments, I realize that I have barely begun to express my gratitude and my debt to a vast community of friends, colleagues and family.

I close with this reminder, "The Lord knows the way through the wilderness. All we have to do is follow." I acknowledge, above all others, the movements of the Holy Spirit in our times and my life that have guided me and lifted me with unending love.

About the Author

Ken is the executive director of *Traces of God*, a spiritual formation ministry founded after his retirement from 40 years of service to American Baptist Churches (ABC/USA). In addition to pastoring churches in Massachusetts and Ohio, he was on the leadership team for national youth events. He led and trained more leaders for an intergenerational spiritual education program called Family Clusters. Ken served on the general board of the ABC, the board of International Ministries and the National Minister's Council.

In 2011 the Lily Endowment awarded Ken a sabbatical grant. During that time, Ken focused his reading, study and travel on building bonds between Christians and Muslims.

Ken's spiritual life was deeply impacted by preaching and evangelism missions to Romania, beginning in 1982. Throughout his ministry Ken led many other short-term mission trips, especially in Latin America. His doctor of ministry program, focused on spiritual formation, led him to write his dissertation on the ways the lives of Christians are transformed by mission. He was invited to seminaries in Mexico to teach on that theme.

Ken has four children and 11 grandchildren. His wife, Kathy, is a stained-glass artist, weaver, gardener and spiritual director. Ken is active at the multi-ethnic church, Sanctuary Columbus, Ohio. He is an avid hiker, woodworker and is currently working on a children's book entitled, *What's Inside An Appleseed?* His first book, *The Extraordinary Ordinary Uplifts Us Halfway to Heaven*, a collection of 52 stories of Ken's encounters with God, also is available at Amazon.com.

Bibliography

Children's Books & Resources

Alex, Marlee, illustrated by Otto Wikkelsoe and Ben Alex, *Grandpa & Me, We Learn About Death*, Scandinavia Publishing House.

Barlow, Connie, Evolutionary Curricula for Children and Youth, http://thegreatstory.org/kids.html

Byers, Grace, illustrated by Keturah A. Bobo, *I Am Enough*, Balzer & Bray HarperCollins.

Cherry, Matthew A., *Hair Love*, Kokila.

Chung, Arree, *Mixed, A Colorful Story*, Henry Holt & Company.

Doerrfeld, Cori, *The Rabbit Listened*, Dial Books for Young Readers.

Fassler, Joan, *My Grandfather Died Today*, Human Sciences Press.

Fox, Karen, illustrated by Nancy Davis, *Older Than the Stars*, Charlesbridge.

Godsey, Maria, illustrated by Christoph J. Kellner, *Not for Me, Please! I Choose to Act Green*, Maria & Joseph Godsey.

Harris, Annaka, illustrated by John Rowe, *I Wonder*, Four Elephants Press.

Hodges, Lynn and Buchanan, Sue, illustrated by John. R. Bendall-Brunello, *I Love You This Much*, Zondervan.

Inches, Allison, illustrated by Pete Whitehead, *The Adventures of a Plastic Bottle: A Story About Recycling*, Little Simon.

Lendler, Ian, illustrated by Shelli Paroline and Braden Lamb, *One Day a Dot: The Story of You, The Universe, and Everything*, First Second.

McBratney, Sam, illustrated by Anita Jeram, *Guess How Much I Love You*, Candlewick Press.

McDonald, Rebecca and James, *I Am Earth*, House of Lore.

McLaren, Brian and Higgins, Gareth, *Cory and the Seventy Story*, The Seventh Story.

Meats, Jeff and Vigil, Izayah, *How Much Do I Love You?*, CreateSpace Publishing Platform.

Morgan, Jennifer, illustrated by Dana Lynne Andersen, *Animals Who Morph: The Universe Tells Our Evolution Story*, Dawn Publications.

Morgan, Jennifer, illustrated by Dana Lynne Andersen, *Born With a Bang: The Universe Tells Our Cosmic Story*, Dawn Publications.

Morgan, Jennifer, illustrated by Dana Lynne Andersen, *From Lava to Life: The Universe Tells Our Earth Story*, Dawn Publications.

Morgan, Jennifer, The Emergent Universe: Books, Storytellings, Programs, Retreats, http://theuniversestory.org

Muhammad, Ibtihaj, illustrated by Hatem Aly, *The Proudest Blue: A Story of Hijab and Family*, Little, Brown and Company.

O'Leary, Sara, illustrated by Qin Leng, *A Family is a Family is a Family*, Groundwood Books.

Rowland, Joanna, illustrated by Thea Baker, *The Memory Box; A Book About Grief*, Sparkhouse Family.

Stillwater, JD, illustrated by Angel Slaughter and Gwen Noll, *Before the Beginning: A Child's First Book of the Great Story*, CreateSpace Publishing Platform.

Thaler, Mike, illustrated by David Wiesner, *Owly*, Walker Books.

Turner, Matthew Paul, illustrated by David Catrow, *When God Made You*, Convergent Books.

Turner, Matthew Paul, illustrated by Gillian Gamble, *When God Made the World*, Convergent Books.

Turner, Matthew Paul, illustrated by Kimberley Barnes, *When I Pray for You*, Convergent Books.

Verde, Susan, illustrated by Peter Reynolds, *I Am Human* (5 book series) Abrams Books for Young Readers.

Verde, Susan, illustrated by Peter Reynolds, *I Am Love: A Book of Compassion*, Abrams Books for Young Readers.

Verde, Susan, illustrated by Peter Reynolds, *I Am Yoga*, Abrams Books for Young Readers.

Spirituality & Science

Bhaumik, Mani, *Code Name God: The Spiritual Odyssey of a Man of Science*, The Crossroad Publishing Company.

Cannato, Judy. *Radical Amazement: Contemplative Lessons from Black Holes, Supernovas, and Other Wonders of the Universe*, Ave Maria Press.

Chopra, Deepak and Mlodinow, Leonard, *War of the Worldviews: Where Science and Spirituality Meet—and Do Not*, Harmony Books.

Dalai Lama, His Holiness, *The Universe in a Single Atom: The Convergence of Science and Spirituality*, Harmony Books.

Dowd, Michael, *Thank God for Evolution: How the Marriage of Science and Religion Will Transform Your Life and Our World*, Plume.

Holmes, Barbara, *Race and the Cosmos*, 2nd edition, CAC Publishing.

Kelsey, Morton, *Encounter with God: A Theology of Christian Experience*, Bethany Fellowship.

Larson, Edward J., *Summer for the Gods: The Scopes Trial and America's Continuing Debate Over Science and Religion*, Basic Books.

Leshan, Lawrence, *The Medium, The Mystic, and the Physicist: Toward a General Theory of the Paranormal*, Allworth.

Lipton, Bruce, *The Biology of Belief: Unleashing the Power of Consciousness, Matter & Miracles*, Hay House Inc.

Phillips, Jan, *No Ordinary Time: The Rise of Spiritual Intelligence and Evolutionary Creativity*, Livingkindness Foundation.

Polkinghorne, John C., *One World: The Interaction of Science and Theology*, Templeton Press.

Sacks, Jonathan, *The Great Partnership: Science, Religion, and the Search for Meaning*, Schocken.

Turner, J. Scott, *Purpose and Desire: What Makes Something "Alive" and Why Modern Darwinism Has Failed to Explain It*, HarperOne.

God & Scripture

Bell, Rob, *Love Wins: A Book About Heaven, Hell, and the Fate of Every Person Who Ever Lived*, HarperOne.

Brueggemann, Walter, *Genesis: Interpretation: A Bible Commentary for Teaching and Preaching*, Westminster John Knox Press.

Collins, Francis, *The Language of God, A Scientist Presents Evidence for Belief*, Free Press.

Davis, Andrew and Clayton, Philip, *How I Found God in Everyone and Everywhere: An Anthology of Spiritual Memoirs*, Monkfish Book Publishing.

Delio, Ilia, *The Unbearable Wholeness of Being: God, Evolution, and the Power of Love*, Orbis Books.

Heschel, Abraham Joshua, *God in Search of Man: A Philosophy of Judaism*, Farrar, Straus and Giroux.

Rollins, Peter, *How (Not) to Speak of God*, Paraclete Press.

Shroyer, Danielle, *Original Blessing: Putting Sin in Its Rightful Place*, Fortress Press.

Smith, Huston, *Why Religion Matters: The Fate of the Human Spirit in an Age of Disbelief*, HarperOne.

Wink, Walter, *The Bible in Human Transformation: Towards a New Paradigm for Biblical Study*, Fortress Press.

Young, Wm. Paul, *Lies We Believe About God*, Atria Books.

Zahnd, Brian, *Sinners in the Hands of a Loving God: The Scandalous Truth of the Very Good News*, WaterBrook.

The Christ, Jesus of Nazareth, Jesus of Faith

Borg, Marcus J., *Jesus: The Life, Teachings and Relevance of a Religious Revolutionary*, HarperOne.

Borg, Marcus J., *Meeting Jesus Again for the First Time: The Historical Jesus and the Heart of Contemporary Faith*, HarperOne.

Bourgeault, Cynthia, *Mystical Hope: Trusting in the Mercy of God*, Cly.

Bourgeault, Cynthia, *The Wisdom Jesus: Transforming Heart and Mind—A New Perspective on Christ and His Message*, Shambhala.

Charleston, Steven, *The Four Vision Quests of Jesus*, Morehouse Publishing.

Delio, Ilia, *Christ In Evolution*, Orbis Books.

Fox, Matthew, *The Coming of the Cosmic Christ: The Healing of Mother Earth and the Birth of a Global Renaissance*, HarperOne.

Lohfink, Gerhard, *No Irrelevant Jesus: On Jesus and the Church Today*, Michael Glazier.

McLaren, Brian D., *A New Kind of Christian: A Tale of Two Friends on a Spiritual Journey*, Jossey-Bass.

McLaren, Brian D., *Everything Must Change: When the World's Biggest Problems and Jesus' Good News Collide*, Thomas Nelson.

McLaren, Brian D., *The Secret Message of Jesus: Uncovering the Truth That Could Change Everything*, Thomas Nelson.

Nolan, Albert, *Jesus Before Christianity*, Orbis Books.

Nolan, Albert, *Jesus Today: A Spirituality of Radical Freedom*, Orbis Books.

Rohr, Richard, *The Divine Dance: The Trinity and Your Transformation*, Whitaker House.

Rohr, Richard, *The Universal Christ: How a Forgotten Reality Can Change Everything We See, Hope For, and Believe*, Convergent Books.

Tickle, Phyllis, *The Great Emergence: How Christianity Is Changing and Why*, Baker Books.

Ethics & Justice

Bray, Melvin, *Better: Waking Up to Who We Could Be*, Chalice Press.

Gushee, David P., *Changing Our Mind: Definitive 3rd Edition of the Landmark Call for Inclusion of LGBTQ Christians with Response to Critics*, Read the Spirit Books.

Kendi, Ibram X, *How to Be An Antiracist*, One World.

Swan, Emily, and Wilson, Ken, *Solus Jesus: A Theology of Resistance*, Read the Spirit Books.

Wink, Walter, *Walter Wink, Collected Readings*, Fortress Press.

Wylie-Kellermann, Bill, *Principalities in Particular: A Practical Theology of the Powers That Be*, Fortress Press.

Resilience & Adaptation

Arnold, J. Heinrich, *Discipleship: Living for Christ in the Daily Grind*, Plough Publishing House.

Baker, Carolyn, *Collapsing Consciously: Transformative Truths for Turbulent Times*, North Atlantic Books.

Burley-Allen, Madelyn, *Listening: The Forgotten Skill*, Wiley.

Batterson, Mark, *Praying Circles Around Your Children*, Zondervan.

Batterson, Mark, *Draw the Circle: The 40 Day Prayer Challenge*, Zondervan.

Bendell, Jem, *Deep Adaptation: A Map for Navigating Climate Tragedy*, IFLAS Occasional Paper 2, July 27, 2018, accessed at www.iflas.info.

Catton, William R., *Overshoot: The Ecological Basis of Revolutionary Change*, University of Illinois Press.

Dowd, Michael, *ProFuture Faith: The Prodigal Species Comes Home*, DVD, Living the Questions.

Delgado, Sharon, *Love in a Time of Climate Change: Honoring Creation, Establishing Justice*, Fortress Press.

Greer, John Michael, *Dark Age America: Climate Change, Cultural Collapse, and the Hard Future Ahead*, New Society Publishers.

Heschel, Abraham J., *Man's Quest for God: Studies in Prayer and Symbolism*, Aurora Press.

Kimmerer, Robin, *Braiding Sweetgrass: Indigenous Wisdom, Scientific Knowledge and the Teachings of Plants*, Milkweed Editions.

Kunstler, James Howard, *Too Much Magic: Wishful Thinking, Technology, and the Fate of the Nation*, Atlantic Monthly Press.

Kunstler, James, *Living In the Long Emergency: Global Crisis, the Failure of the Futurists, and the Early Adapters Who Are Showing Us the Way Forward*, BenBella Books.

Kunstler, James, *World Made By Hand* (A series of four novels), Atlantic Monthly Press.

LeBlanc, Miriam, *Easter Stories: Classic Tales for the Holy Season*, Plough Publishing House.

Lerch, Daniel, *Community Resilience Reader, Essential Resources for An Era of Upheaval*, Island Press.

Louv, Richard, *Last Child in the Woods; Saving Our Children from Nature-Deficit Disorder*, Algonquin Books.

Macy, Joanna, and Johnstone, Chris, *Active Hope: How to Face the Mess We're in without Going Crazy*, New World Library.

Macy, Joanna, and Brown, Molly, *Coming Back to Life: The Updated Guide to the Work That Reconnects*, New Society Publishers.

Mackenzie, Don, Falcon, Ted, and Rahman, Jamal, *Finding Peace through Spiritual Practice: The Interfaith Amigo's Guide to Personal, Social and Environmental Healing*, Skylight Paths.

Meyer, William, *Three Breaths and Begin: A Guide to Meditation in the Classroom*, New World Library.

Moore, Charles, *Called to Community: The Life Jesus Wants for His People*, Plough Publishing House.

Peterson, Eugene H., *Answering God: The Psalms as Tools for Prayer*, HarperOne.

Rollins, Peter, *The Divine Magician: The Disappearance of Religion and the Discovery of Faith*, Howard Books.

Swimme, Brian Thomas, *Hidden Heart of the Cosmos: Humanity and the New Story*, Orbis Books.

Swimme, Brian, and Berry, Thomas *The Universe Story: From the Primordial Flaring Forth to the Ecozoic Era—A Celebration of the Unfolding of the Cosmos*, HarperOne.

Tucker, Mary, Grim John, and Angyal, Andrew, *Thomas Berry: A Biography*, Columbia University Press.

Wicks, Robert, *Night Call: Embracing Compassion and Hope in a Troubled World*, Oxford University Press.

Wicks, Robert, *Spiritual Resilience: 30 Days to Refresh Your Soul*, Franciscan Media.